PLAY A **BIGGER** GAME

PLAY A BIGGER GAME

HOW TO
ACHIEVE MORE
BE MORE
DO MORE
HAVE MORE

Rowdy McLean

WILEY

First published in 2012 by
John Wiley & Sons Australia, Ltd
42 McDougall St, Milton Qld 4064

Reprinted with corrections 2017

Office also in Melbourne

Typeset in 11pt/13.5pt

© Rowdy McLean 2012

The moral rights of the author have been asserted.

National Library of Australia Cataloguing-in-Publication data:

Author:	McLean, Rowdy.
Title:	Play a bigger game: how to achieve more, be more, do more, have more / Rowdy McLean.
ISBN:	9780730344810 (pbk.)
Subjects:	Self-realisation. Conduct of life.
Dewey Number:	158.1

Author photograph by Shae Style Photography

Printed in Australia by Ligare Book Printer

10 9 8 7 6 5 4 3 2 1

Disclaimer

The material in this publication is of the nature of general comment only, and does not represent professional advice. It is not intended to provide specific guidance for particular circumstances and it should not be relied on as the basis for any decision to take action or not take action on any matter which it covers. Readers should obtain professional advice where appropriate, before making any such decision. To the maximum extent permitted by law, the author and publisher disclaim all responsibility and liability to any person, arising directly or indirectly from any person taking or not taking action based on the information in this publication.

This book is dedicated to my mum, Chrissy, for encouraging me to play a bigger game in my life, for her belief that I could do it and for the reality checks when I got too big for my boots. This is also for all the mums who give so much of themselves so their children can achieve more, be more, do more and have more.

Foreword

This book is the real deal: let me tell you why.

Okay, you bought the book. Big deal. I stopped long ago being impressed with people who buy books. Buying a book won't make you better. It might make you temporarily feel better but your life won't change much. I have written five bestsellers and sold hundreds of thousands of books and I can assure you that not one person who ever bought one of my books is any better off simply for buying it.

But you didn't just buy the book. You actually took the next step. You opened up your book and are now reading the foreword. Good for you. You are further along than many but you are still just pretty average. I say that because the average person who buys a book gets this far. So I'm still not impressed. The average person will read the front and back cover, the foreword and even get through the first couple of chapters, and then their interest tapers off. They get busy doing other things. Then they lay the book aside with the intention of getting back to it...someday. Bottom line: they give up and quit. It's not the book's fault; it's their own fault. That's because the average person just can't stick with anything long enough to enjoy the results.

Average people get average results because they do average things. And on average, most people will start a project — a diet, a plan, or even a book — and after taking a few steps in the right direction will then slide off the path.

They never achieve what they set out to achieve. They never reach their dreams. They never get rich. They never have amazing relationships. They never do incredible things.

I can't stand those people.

Too many people have settled for less than their best and it makes me sick. If you give something your very best effort and then end up with average results, then I will cut you some slack. But I don't believe that's how it works. I don't buy that average results come from anyone's best effort. Yet that is what people accept and settle for. So here's a word of advice for you: don't.

Do not settle. Don't accept less than your own personal best. Don't be average. Instead, right now, make an above average decision: decide to make it all the way to the end of this great little book. Decide to stop talking about success and actually become successful. Decide to *play a bigger game!*

That's what you are ready to do, right? You are ready to play a bigger game so your life will look better going forward than it has been when you look backward. At least you said that was what you wanted when you bought this book.

I can assure you that you have come to right place. This book can give you what it takes to reach the top. It can move you from average to outstanding. And it's written in such a way that you won't have any excuses left when you reach the end.

This is not your typical 'I'm going to teach you how to be successful' crap by a guy who isn't successful. Rowdy is the real deal. And, best of all, Rowdy actually plays a bigger game! He lives it. It shows in everything he does. It's the very essence of who he really is. I admire that: a guy who walks his talk. And trust me, there aren't many people I can say that about. Rowdy is the real deal.

So if you are tired of average, tired of having less, being less, doing less and achieving less, it's time to get ROWDY! Rowdy can put energy back in your life. He can give you the insights and the plan to put mediocrity behind you and play a bigger game!

Larry Winget
Five-time bestselling author and television personality
Author of *The Wall Street Journal* #1 bestseller, *Shut Up,*
Stop Whining and Get a Life

Contents

About the author

Playing a Bigger Game has been Rowdy McLean's life story. A successful, yet down to earth, entrepreneur and business leader, Rowdy retired at 34, became bored and got back in the game, creating new companies (that he still owns and runs today) and turning others around.

He now helps organisations, teams and individuals play a bigger game, in business, leadership and life.

As an international keynote speaker Rowdy presents at conferences and events across the globe as well as running corporate immersions, single or multi day master classes, executive mentoring programs and facilitating offsite meetings and retreats.

Rowdy has spoken to over 250000 people in the USA, Europe, Asia and Australia. His book *Play a Bigger Game* has been published in 7 countries.

An adventurer at heart, Rowdy has climbed Mt Kilimajaro, kayaked in Antarctica and tracked gorillas in Rwanda. He has played professional rugby league, run marathons, spent time on the Serengeti with the Masaii warriors and regularly takes leaders up into the heart of Arnhem Land.

Rowdy has a Masters Degree in Business Administration and is a graduate of the Disney Institute. He is a fellow of the Australian Institute of Management, the Customer Service Institute of Australia, and recipient of the Certified Speaking Professional designation (the highest honour awarded to speakers across the globe).

QR codes

As a bonus, an exclusive video has been developed for each chapter of the book.

To help you get the most out of *Play a Bigger Game* we have provided a QR code at the end of every chapter. These codes are linked to exclusive videos and other resources. If you want to know more about QR codes, simply scan the code below with your phone or visit our website:

www.playabiggergame.com.au/play-a-bigger-game/qrcodes.

If you don't have a QR code compatible mobile phone, you can still access all the extra features by visiting the URL—for example, for chapter 1, www.playabiggergame.com.au/chapter1.

The QR code, or Quick Response Code, is a mobile phone readable barcode. Some mobile phones come equipped with QR code; others require you to download a QR reader app. The easiest way to test if your phone has a pre-installed QR code is to point your phone's camera at the QR code. If the device has decoding software installed, it will fire up its browser and go straight to that URL. If not, simply download any QR reader onto your phone then pass the phone's camera over the barcode.

Setting up for success

You have probably picked up this book believing that it contains information that will help you get more out of life. Let me assure you that it will do exactly that, but there is something you can do that will greatly boost your chances of getting what you want from this book, and from life. You need to prepare yourself for what's inside.

Playing a bigger game is all about seizing the opportunity to *achieve more*, *be more*, *do more* and *have more* than you ever thought was possible. Let's take just a few minutes to explore what that means. It won't take long and will increase your chances of success tenfold. So grab a pen and a pad and get set to make some quick notes. It has been shown that 60 per cent of people who purchase a personal development book never finish it. Even fewer do anything with the information. I want this book to be different. That's why it's short and to the point, and broken down into simple steps that anyone can follow. The reason most people fail to follow through is that they fail to prepare properly. A few minutes' preparation will make a world of difference to your results, and results are what matters.

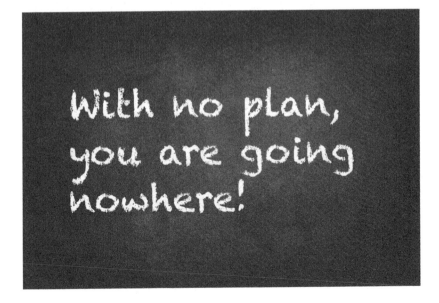

With no plan, you are going nowhere!

To prepare for the journey this book will take you on, you need to understand your goals: specifically in what ways do you want to *achieve more*, *be more* and *do more*, and what exactly do you want to *have more* of? If you are not sure of the answers to these questions, how can you possibly create a plan to go out and get it. So let's look at them in more detail.

Achieve more

Achieving more is about success. It's about what you would like to be a winner at. Success means different things to different people. To someone with no money it could be getting a job; to someone with a million dollars it could be turning that into 10 million. It could be winning a trophy or becoming a champion, employee of the month or head of your department. It could be winning the race or just running the race. You know what success means to you at this stage of your life. Take a minute to jot down some notes about what *achieving more*, or success, means to you.

Success means different things to different people.

Be more

We play many different roles in life. *Being more* is about how we show up in these roles. Consider for a second all the roles you play. You may be a parent, partner, friend, colleague, employee, employer, boss, neighbour, community member, to name just a few. Write down the roles that are important to you and why you would like to *be more* in that role. Perhaps you don't spend as much time with your kids as you should or maybe you are disconnected from your friends. Describe what needs to change.

Your thoughts don't make you a better person. Your actions do!

Do more

All of us have at some time made a new year's resolution or a bucket list of all the things we would like to do. *Doing more* is about the experiences you want to have and the things you want to do. Make a list of the things you would really like to do in the next 12 months. It could be to go to Paris, learn Spanish, run the New York marathon or give up smoking. You get the idea. Quickly write down your bucket list for the next 12 months.

> Your have to have something exciting to anchor yourself to in your future!

Have more

Having more is about ownership, or what belongs to us. So it could relate to how much money you want to have in the bank, the type of car or house you own, the clothes or jewellery you wear, your boat or even your pets. What are the things you would like to have in your life in the next 12 months. Ownership is not just about material things, though. We also 'own' our reputation, for instance; indeed, for some people their reputation is more important than any material possession. What sort of reputation would you like to have? What would you like to be remembered for?

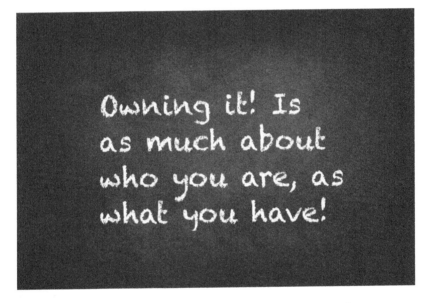

Owning it! Is as much about who you are, as what you have!

So that's it. If you have completed that quick exercise you are ready to play a bigger game and have massively increased your chances of success. In fact, if you really did complete the exercise give yourself a pat on the back, as you are *already* playing a bigger game, because I can assure you that most people didn't do it. If you didn't do it, go back and do it now. It will be worth it!

Introduction

We all want more! More money, more fun, more love, more time, more friends, more adventure, more holidays. This book is for those people who want more, and want it *now!*

If you have reached a state of supreme happiness. If you have all the material possessions you could possibly muster. If you are absolutely the best person you can possibly be. If you are in the peak of health. And if every single one of your relationships is full of all the respect, trust and love you could hope for, then close this book and put it back on the shelf or pass it on to someone else.

If, on the other hand, you are in search of more freedom and fulfilment, if you want to raise the bar, push the boundaries and reach a higher level, then keep reading.

This book is about giving you the simple tools and strategies to achieve more, be more, do more and have more. If you use these tools and strategies you will be able to play a bigger game—a much bigger game. I can promise you that if you follow the strategies in this book, if you actually act on them, rather than just reading about them, you will get more out of life than you ever imagined.

Playing a **bigger** game is choosing to **stretch** yourself.

Life is a wonderful adventure. Note that I use the word *adventure*—I don't say life is easy. To get more out of life, you are going to have to stretch a little, or maybe a lot. You're going to have to go through some pain, give up some of your current comforts and put in some effort.

I can guarantee that, if you really want it and are prepared to put in the effort, absolutely 110 per cent, it will be worth it. The wonder of life is in the adventure. The journey is marked with events and milestones that teach you to be better, to be stronger and to be more courageous. It is in the journey that we learn to achieve more, be more, do more and have more—and, trust me, you can and you will!

It is in the **journey** that we learn to achieve **more**, be **more**, do **more** and have **more**—and, trust me, you can and you will!

But let's take a reality check right here, right now. If you don't really want more out of life, if you have everything you want or need; if you have made your mark in life and are happy with how your contribution will measure up in history; if you have made all the big plays, participated in the biggest games and are satisfied with the outcomes, then give this book to a friend or colleague or someone that needs it more than you. If, on the other hand, you still have a desire to do things, go places, make a difference and realise your maximum potential; if you are prepared to push the envelope, squeeze every last drop out of the game of life; if you truly want to play a much, much bigger game, then read on.

And you have permission to be confused at times. In fact, confusion is the highest state of learning. If at any stage in the book you find yourself thinking, 'I just don't get it!', that's good because something in your mind is vibrating around the problem, 'How do I get it? How do I sort this out for myself?' It means you will actually be learning as you read. So feel free to be confused sometimes. I guarantee all the pieces of the puzzle will come together long before the end of the book.

> You have no idea
> of what you are
> capable of, until
> you play all in!

Who wants to be average? Definitely not you or you would not have picked up this book in the first place. I have written *Play a Bigger Game* knowing you will not want to settle for less than what is truly possible in your life. After lots of mistakes and some not so good experiences in my life, I now know the rules to playing a bigger game, and this book has given me an opportunity to share them with you.

The path to an **awesome** life is **playing** a bigger game.

Playing a bigger game means continually looking for the very best version of you in everything you do. It's looking for opportunities, developing your potential and growing in awesome ways you never imagined possible. It's taking every aspect of your existence and refining, reviewing and reinventing it. It's not sitting on the sidelines wishing you were in the game. It's getting on the team and being the most valuable player and creating an end game that will make you proud of the score line.

So come with me as I show you how to play a bigger game in your life and how to *achieve more*, *be more*, *do more* and *have more*.

Rowdy McLean

Chapter 1
Break out of the cotton wool society

Today we live in a cotton wool society and I am over it! There are so many rules, so many regulations and so many people telling us what we can and can't do. You go to the beach and there are signs telling you don't run, don't rollerblade, don't fish, don't skate, no bikes, no phones, no cars, no alcohol—essentially no fun! Don't swim, don't run, don't walk, don't talk, don't eat, don't drink. There are all these things you can't do. You go to work and you've got occupational health and safety rules, all these human resource regulations, risk management. Stop doing this, start doing that, don't go here, don't go there. All the things we can't do, but not much about what we can do. We get caught up in all the *cant's* and it stops us from stepping out and stepping up. We get so used to constantly being told where to be and what to do that we lose the ability to take charge of our own lives, to be responsible for our own behaviours, results and outcomes.

It seems to me the world has gone crazy! We create more rules to protect people from harm and try to influence their behaviour. Some of these things border on the ridiculous: schools ban kids from turning cartwheels; proposed laws require you to walk your dog; teeth cleaning is mandated in daycare centres; licences are required for just about everything from fishing to busking.

> Life should be
> a wonderful
> daring adventure,
> that is both,
> remarkable and
> memorable!

Within this cotton wool protection, we are too afraid to take up the adventure of life because we have all these people telling us we can't go there, we shouldn't do it, we shouldn't try it, we shouldn't give it a go.

More and more people are living their lives vicariously through watching reality television shows. We watch *MasterChef* but eat fast food. We watch *The Biggest Loser* rather than go to the gym. We would rather watch *Survivor* than set out on our own adventure, and rather watch *The Apprentice* than start a business ourselves. Then we get nice and comfy on the lounge and we watch Jerry Springer just to prove to ourselves that, compared with others, our lives aren't really that stuffed up.

We have become a nation of watchers, not doers.

The cotton wool society holds us back, putting us in boxes and applying labels that define us by our actions. From the day we're born we are labelled: he cries a lot, she sleeps a lot, so there we are in our first box. Then we go to school and we get put in more boxes: she is good at sport; he is disruptive; she can dance. Then we go to work and get put in another box: he is not a team player; she doesn't write good reports; he is not dedicated. Throughout life we are given more and more labels and are put into more and more boxes. The cotton wool society shapes the way we live. Everyone is expected to do things the same way and we get caught in this system and pattern.

The great achievers in life don't fit into the boxes. They won't accept being put inside a box or accept being labelled. They shrug it off. They create their own path and take responsibility for their own lives and results.

Are you living in a system of same old, same old, doing what everyone else does? It goes something like this: I'm born. I live in a family in a certain degree of financial security. I grow up in that family. I go to school. I go out into the wide world and look for a job. I find a partner. Everyone asks me when I'm going to have kids, so I have kids, and everyone wants to know when we are having another. Then everyone asks when I'm going to get a new job. The family is on my back about when we're going to get a bigger house, a better car. Living life in this cotton wool society, you grow to believe that you need to do all these things in this way, following the same pattern.

Then you get to the stage when life is starting to run out, and you ask yourself, 'What am I going to do when I retire?' Then you retire, get a watch in a gift box, and do very little until you are put in your final box—and that's the end of it. I don't know about you but I refuse to live in these boxes. I refuse to accept the labels. I refuse to do the things that average people do. I refuse to participate in a world that has decided to watch rather than do.

Don't get me started on the people who use social media throughout the day to register the non-events in their boring lives—every move they make! 'just had a long flat white coffee with two sugars at Lala restaurant'; 'just parked the car at qvb car park'. Do they really think anyone cares enough about their daily life to read all these silly messages? Isn't it time they got a life and played a bigger game than they are currently playing? Did something remarkable or amazing? Created a life that was outstanding and then sent some messages about that you would really like to read?

I think we need to break out of the cotton wool society and create a different path, a path paved with enthusiasm, excitement and adventure, where we enjoy every possible moment, a path rich with rewards of happiness and fulfilment. Something absolutely awesome and amazing.

It's time we took charge of our own welfare. It's time we took responsibility for our own decisions, our own behaviour and, ultimately, the consequences and outcomes of our lives.

I'm fortunate in my life. I get to mentor CEOs, work with successful leaders and teams and the highest of high achievers. I also get to work with people and organisations that are stuck in a rut and going nowhere. I work with sportspeople and with schoolchildren. Most importantly, I get the opportunity to have many conversations with them about the difference between *average* and *awesome*.

When I talk to outstanding achievers, amazing teams and awesome organisations, they all say the same thing: there are two paths we can choose.

There are **two paths** that we can choose—the path of **average** or the path of **awesome**.

We can choose the path of average, which is very crowded, full of people caught up in the cotton wool society just doing enough to get by. They play safe: 'We don't want to get outside that cotton wool, or get caught up in something that might be a little bit risky, a little bit dangerous and a little bit adventurous, a little bit out of our comfort zone—even for a day.'

The second path is the path to an awesome life, the path to playing a bigger game. There are very few people, teams and organisations on the path to awesome. Why is that? Could it be because you have to do a little bit more, to make a bit more of an effort? You have to get outside that cotton wool, get outside your comfort zone and do things other people are not prepared to do.

Sourena—no limits

Sourena Vasseghi is a guy who just refuses to let the cotton wool society shape what he does and how he does it. Society is quick to label people like Sourena and loves to put them in boxes, tell them what they can and can't do.

You see, at the age of two Sourena was diagnosed with cerebral palsy, but he just refused to accept the limitations that society believes should be placed on his life. In fact, he has broken all the rules. In 2001 he graduated from the University of Southern California with a business and marketing degree and opened his own marketing firm. He has written an award-winning book, *Love Your Life and It Will Love You Back*. These days he travels the country with his good friend Rich Finley, sharing his story and motivating others to live a life outside the cotton wool society.

If a guy like Sourena can find the courage to stare the cotton wool society in the face and say 'No way', I am sure any of us can take the opportunity to step outside of the box and see what happens.

Chapter 1 summary

- ✍ We live in a cotton wool society that keeps us inside our comfort zone and puts us in boxes.

- ✍ The great achievers in life don't fit into boxes.

- ✍ We need to break out of the cotton wool society and create a different path that is paved with enthusiasm, excitement and adventure.

- ✍ We need to take responsibility for our own welfare and results.

- ✍ There are two paths we can choose: the path of average or the path of awesome.

My game plan (don't skip this—it's important)

Most people who read this book won't do anything with the insights and ideas it inspires (sad, but unfortunately true). Let me tell you why. Most people will turn to the next chapter without pausing long enough to capture their ideas and thoughts. Yes, I know what you're thinking: I'll come back and do it later. *No you won't.* So stop right now and take a few minutes to write down your ideas—your personal game plan. You don't want to write inside a new book? Build a bridge, get over it. This book is about getting you better results, so you need a better plan. That's where the 'My game plan' page becomes extremely useful. Capturing your personal thoughts at the end of each chapter will help you build up your personal plan step by step. These notes will be invaluable to you in the future. So do it, don't turn to the next chapter till it's done. Even if it's just one idea it'll set you on your way to playing a bigger game.

MY GAME PLAN:

....

....

....

....

....

....

....

....

....

....

....

....

....

....

....

....

....

....

....

....

....

....

....

....

....

....

....

....

....

....

Chapter 2
Play a **bigger**
game!

So what does playing a bigger game mean? It means choosing to stretch yourself:

- 👍 to test the boundaries
- 👍 to become better
- 👍 to achieve greater things
- 👍 to be a better person
- 👍 to do things you have never done before
- 👍 to have things in your life you never thought possible.

There are some myths in today's society about playing a bigger game — some ideas that are promoted as shortcuts to winning anything and everything you want.

There is the myth about the power of positive thinking. Perhaps you have read that book? All you have to do is be positive, just be positive all the time and life is going to be great. Think positive all the time and life will turn out just the way you want it to.

That is just rubbish and I refuse to believe it. There are two things wrong with positive thinking on its own. The first is that you just cannot be positive all the time; it's pretty much impossible to do.

Imagine you are buying a new car. Think about the type of a car you want to buy, how good it looks all brand new, bright and shiny. Now imagine you have taken it home, parked it out the front and are ready to show it to your family. As you walk inside, a young kid comes skateboarding down the hill and slips, kicking the skateboard up in the air and boom, right into the side of your new car, scraping off a big chunk of paint.

How is your positive thinking going right now?

How are you going to react? Are you going to groan and express disappointment and annoyance, just for a few minutes? Of course you are. It's okay to be negative! You just don't want to *live* in that space. You don't want to be the person who has got their finger stuck in the bug zapper of life, constantly frazzled and frowning.

You know people, I'm sure, who live in the negative. They struggle to find anything good in life. They complain about everything, from the programs on television and the price of food to the weather, the traffic and parking—too hot, too cold, too tired, too busy. They never have a positive word or a constructive comment to make. Sure, let off some steam, be real about things, but don't let negative sentiments control your life.

The second problem with positive thinking is that on its own it doesn't create anything—it's just thoughts. I read a book recently that had apparently sold thousands of copies. It's message was simple: what you think about all day long, you become. Following this logic, if you lie on the lounge eating donuts, watching soap operas and thinking about a million dollars all day long, you will become a millionaire. I don't think so.

I believe you can become what you think about all day long *if* you also take action to make it a reality. So if you are thinking about having a million dollars and you also act to make that a reality, there is a good chance it will happen. Positive thinking combined with positive action is far more likely to get results than positive thinking alone.

On the journey to playing a bigger game some people get stuck on the path of average and end up in places like If Only. In the town of If Only, you will find lots of people who talk up a storm, who are going to do all these wonderful things, but they never actually get around to it. They're the ones who are always saying:

- 👍 If only I had gone there.
- 👍 If only I had got that promotion.
- 👍 If only I had married her/him.
- 👍 If only I had taken that opportunity.
- 👍 If only I had tried this or that.

If Only is a place leading nowhere, and the town next door is called Luck. People on the path of average believe that Luck is a great place to be. They wish for life to be simple; they want to have it really easy. So they think luck is a strategy in life. If they buy enough lottery tickets sooner or later they're going to have everything they want. If they just hope hard enough they'll become winners.

I know a guy called Brendan who is always telling everyone that life is going to get so much better when he wins the lottery. It's his typical response to just about anything: 'She'll be right. I'm going to win the lottery, and then life will be awesome.' I ran into him last week and he gave me the same old line. So this time I asked him how many tickets he had in this week's lottery.

'Tickets? I haven't bought any tickets for months,' he said. How is he going to win the lottery if he doesn't even buy a ticket? The good things in life don't show up if you don't participate. I know Brendan's chances of winning the lottery are not great even if he has a ticket, but if you're not participating, you have absolutely no chance.

Brendan is a 'leave it to luck' sort of guy. He wants to have an awesome life but he also wants it to be easy. He wants to take the shortcuts that go with having an average life.

Even the people who think luck is a strategy have to get off their backsides and do something. They have to go and buy the ticket, they have to turn up. The reality is that luck is not a strategy; if you really want a better life you need to do something about it, not just gamble on it getting better.

In the same little valley as If Only and Luck there is also a place called Can't. In the town of Can't people justify not playing a bigger game by using defensive statements. They will often say to themselves:

- 🖒 I could do that if I wanted to but I can't find the time.

- 🖒 I could honestly have that job but I just can't put myself through the process of applying for it.

- 🖒 I could have an awesome business, but I just can't be bothered to put the time and effort into making it happen.

- 🖒 I could have all the things I want but I just can't commit to what it takes to get them.

In the town of Can't people give up on their hopes and dreams because they will not break out of the cotton wool world.

Just down the road from Can't is the town of Won't. You will recognise these people by their language:

- 🖒 I won't do it because you're pushing me.

- 🖒 I won't lose weight because that's someone else's idea.

- 🖒 I won't start that business up because you suggested it and I didn't think of it myself.

These people think that pushing back is the way forward, but in fact they're not going anywhere.

The last town in that valley is Gonna (translation: *I am going to*). How many Gonna people do you know in your life today? You know, those people who are always gonna change the world but never get around to it.

I love the Gonnas. In January, at the start of a new year, the Gonnas are out in full force. You will regularly hear them say:

🖒 This year I'm gonna do this, I'm gonna do that.

🖒 This year I'm gonna lose a whole heap of weight.

🖒 This year I'm gonna get that new job.

🖒 This year I'm gonna travel around the world.

You bump into them the following December and ask how things are going, and believe it or not, nothing has changed. We have the same conversations: 'Next year I'm gonna do this and I'm gonna do that.' But you know that in reality it's all talk, the Gonnas never get anything done.

So the very crowded valley of Average, where you find the towns of If Only, Luck, Can't, Won't and Gonna, is like a big merry-go-round, with endless circling but no beginning or ending—just the same old, same old. Week after week, year after year, the average pattern is continually repeated. Some people live in Average valley all their lives, only to realise too late that there are many other exciting places out there where they could have lived, or even visited from time to time. If you grow old in Average valley, most of your conversations when you are sitting on the verandah in your rocking chair will start with 'I wish'—I wish I had tried this; I wish I had done that; I wish I had gone there. People who live in those towns all use an excuse strategy; they will never play a bigger game.

If you want to play a bigger game, you have to move out of Average, leave those towns and the people in them behind, and start the new adventure. Average people will discourage you from trying to change your habits, language and actions or from aiming higher. One of their greatest fears is that in playing a bigger game (and secretly they know you will succeed) you will make them look bad and force them to admit to their excuse strategy and actually step up to the plate themselves—with no excuses. They are truly afraid of playing a bigger game, and hanging out with them and their negativity may be keeping you small!

Unfortunately, some of these excuse makers may be members of your immediate family, neighbours or long-time friends. Knowing that the only person you can change is *you*, don't waste your time and energy trying to change others. Focus on *you*. When *you* get better, the game gets bigger.

That doesn't mean you drop all your old friends—that would be silly. But maybe you can find a way to spend a little less time with them. Change the conversation regularly when they go into 'excuse mode'. Become more aware of how easy it is to hook into negativity when you are surrounded by people going nowhere on the path of average.

Cadel—playing to win

Getting back on the bike proved to be a good strategy for Cadel Evans. For a cyclist, the greatest event you can compete in is the *Tour de France*, a grinding race of attrition over 14 days through some of the toughest terrain imaginable. It takes the riders across France and neighbouring countries via the famous Alps, where many a contender finds the true meaning of strength, commitment and determination—and the true experience of exhaustion. Often referred to as the 'tour of truth', the contest challenges riders on every possible level.

Australian Cadel Evans managed to come second in this amazing race in both 2007 and 2008. It would have been easy for him to decide that he had played his biggest game, given it his best shot. A lot of people would have been happy to settle for two seconds in such a big race but not Cadel. For him winning was the bigger game and in 2011, at the age of 34, he became the oldest winner of the world's most competitive bike race. Now, that's a bigger game!

Chapter 2 summary

- 🖒 Playing a bigger game is choosing to stretch yourself.
- 🖒 There are no shortcuts.
- 🖒 Don't let negativity control your life.

👍 You can become what you think about *and act on*.

👍 Some people live in Average valley all their lives.

MY GAME PLAN:

....

....

....

....

....

....

....

....

....

....

Play a bigger game!

....

....

....

....

....

....

....

....

....

....

....

....

....

....

....

17

Chapter 3
You are awesome!

Picture this: you're standing at the bottom of a snow-covered mountain. The sun is just coming over the peaks. There are shadows in the valleys and you're looking up. Down the mountain comes a snowboarder in a bright pink suit, blonde hair flying back behind her. She's going up one side and cutting big curves, coming down through the shadows and back up the other side. She's going flat out down this mountain being chased by someone else.

She comes flying down to the bottom where you are, spins the snowboard around, sprays a plume of snow up in the air, kicks off the board, lifts it above her head, and jumps up and down shouting 'Yes, yes, yes!!!' You just stand there watching then walk over to her and ask, 'How was that?' She replies, 'Awesome, absolutely awesome. That was an awesome run!'

The way to change an average life into an awesome life is to create more awesome moments than average moments. We all have awesome moments, don't we? You know, when you've stepped up to the plate, you've done the right thing and you've done more than enough. You have got out there and feel really good. Your blood pumps, your skin tingles and you feel 10 foot tall and bulletproof. Don't you love those moments? Just like the girl in the story above, you feel the excitement and thrill of pushing the boundaries and challenging yourself, and the exhilaration of getting through it, achieving success.

We all have average moments too. Those moments when you want the ground to swallow you up, when you feel sick in the stomach, when you haven't done enough or you haven't done the right thing. I've had some really awesome moments and lots of very average ones too.

I remember as a young guy growing up in a little country town in northern New South Wales. My mates and I used to go up to the local football ground and collect the soft drink bottles that were dropped out of the cars. We would take those soft drink bottles down to Nick's Café on Main Street and would trade them for 5 cents each. Then we would buy a few cokes and a bag of chips and head back up to the footy ground and collect some more bottles to take down to Nick's.

One day we were at the café collecting our small change from Nick. As we walked out, my mate said, 'You know what? All that Nick does with those bottles is he puts them out the back'. I know what you're thinking, and that's what I thought too—this is my start as an entrepreneur!

So we waited a little while, walked round the back and climbed over the fence and passed the bottles over to our mates. We then waited a little longer, took the bottles around the front and traded the same bottles to Nick for 5 cents each. I thought, 'Is this a great business opportunity or what?'

When it was my turn to climb over the fence, I'm there passing the bottles over and I hear a big clunk on the ground on the other side. I thought that was strange and when I passed over the next one the same thing happened. So I put my head over to see what was happening on the other side of the fence.

Standing on the other side of the fence was Sergeant Wilkins. This was back in the day when policemen were really big. Sergeant Jeff Wilkins, 7 feet, 8 inches tall, two pick handles across the shoulders. Size 17 boots. You know how I know the size? He used one to kick me up the backside and sent me home to my father, who decided that kick was a great idea and gave me a matching one.

> # A kick in the pants, is lifes way of telling you to Play A Bigger Game!

Average moment? You bet. When I looked over that fence, I wanted the ground to swallow me up. I felt sick in the stomach. I knew I had done the wrong thing. I knew I hadn't stepped up to the plate. I knew I had taken a shortcut in the game of life. I knew it was an average thing to do. The kick in the backside made me resolve never to choose to do the average thing again.

We do that, don't we? We take short cuts, we don't do the things we should, we sometimes don't experience life in the way we should. Our days are filled with opportunities for awesome and average moments, and we decide in a split second, many times a day, what our outcomes will be. If we are aiming to play a bigger game, our choices are much clearer. I have absolutely no doubt that you are capable of far more than you imagine. I truly believe it. Let me tell you why.

You are **awesome**.

I am yet to meet a person in my life who is not awesome, but there are plenty of people I have met who have just not discovered it for themselves—yet.

Though you may think of yourself as only average, you are in fact the latest in a long line of success stories. Your ancestors have been fast enough, smart enough, strong enough and courageous enough to survive thousands of years of famine, plague, predators, ice ages and extreme weather events, and every generation has been more awesome than the previous generation.

You've got the most complex audio-visual system on the planet. Your eyes can recognise 10 million different colours. Your nose can identify 10 000 different smells. You have 97 000 kilometres of capillaries running through your body. You have a pump in your chest that beats 100 000 times a day every single day for about 80 years. You have a computer in your head that has 30 billion cells capable of processing a million bits of information in a second, much faster than the latest computers or iPads.

You are awesome.

Just 200 years ago the average lifespan in the western world was 35 years. Today it has doubled to more than 70. Humans can run 100 metres in 9 seconds, run for hours without stopping, climb mountains, swim great distances, leap over 9.144 metres, calculate complex equations and solve problems of monumental complexity.

In the twentieth century alone humanity invented antibiotics, plastics, electricity, aeroplanes, nuclear reactors, atomic bombs, genetics, transistors, television, computers, the internet, electronics, airconditioning, many medicines, microwaves, movies, automobiles, teflon, ultrasonic flight, skyscrapers, manned space flights, mobile phones and iPods, to name just a few, and there are many more amazing things to come.

You are **awesome**.

You are the greatest engine ever built, and the sooner you put that engine to work, the more awesome you will be! I believe the greatest waste in the entire world is the waste of human potential. This book is designed to help you discover and act on *your* potential and allow you to create and realise your dreams.

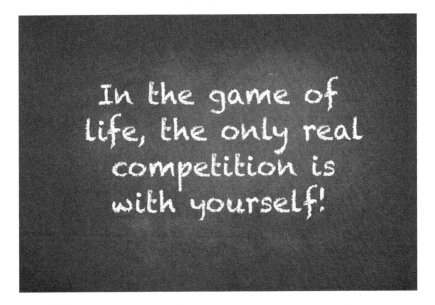

In writing this book I want to ignite a flame under you, a flame that will compel you to step up, raise the bar and start on the journey to playing a bigger game.

Have you ever thought about just how awesome you are? No, seriously. You should take the time to stop, look in the mirror and tell yourself you are amazing. You are an amazing package of potential just waiting to make things happen.

The **greatest** waste in the **world** is the waste of **potential**.

Just being alive is awesome. You're capable of more than any other living being on the planet. You can experience emotions, feelings, you can run, jump, swim, write, sing and draw. The only thing you can't do is fly, but we have even found a way around that. So you're awesome. You're awesome before you even begin.

And sometimes the thing that holds us back in this cotton wool society is the belief that we're not good enough. 'I'm not capable enough.' 'It might work for someone else but not for me.' Yet when you stop to think, the reality is you are just as capable as anyone else. We all have 24 hours in a day. What shapes us as individuals is how much life we put into that 24 hours. Time is the real differentiator. We all get the same supply; its what you do with it that sets you apart from the rest of the population. Think about how awesome, fantastic and absolutely amazing you are right now, and we haven't even begun to play a bigger game yet.

What do you want to happen in the future? And how can you make that happen? The ball is in your court. As you work your way through the exercises in this book and put the ideas into practice, your life will be changed.

In 12 months you will be amazed by your achievements, and in five years' time you will look back through this book and think, 'Oh my goodness, I have achieved some amazing things and had a remarkable journey because...

- 👍 I have choice.
- 👍 I am clever.
- 👍 I am unique.
- 👍 I am capable.
- 👍 I get things done.
- 👍 I am creative.

👍 I am awesome.

👍 I got off my backside.

👍 I made a difference.'

Sarah — down but not out

I met Sarah at an event in New York.

She talked to me about playing a bigger game, about feeling she had lost her way in life, and confided that she lacked the enthusiasm and energy to push the boundaries or stretch herself. She was stuck in a rut, inside her comfort zone, going nowhere and not at all happy.

Meeting her again the following year at an event in Sydney, I learned things were even worse. She had left her job and was sleeping on the floor of a one-bedroom apartment with a milk crate as her only piece of furniture.

She had lost her belief in herself. We spent some time discussing her capabilities and what she was awesome at and then started the process of building her confidence. For Sarah, it was a matter of taking small steps.

The first one was to borrow some furniture, a huge step for her. Sarah felt as though she was begging and found the whole exercise humiliating, but she did it. We then worked out the next best step for her and she followed through on that. We continued in this way, one step at a time.

Before long Sarah had her own consulting business, employed two staff and moved into a cool office in a trendy part of town.

We have been working together now for more than 10 years, each year playing the game a little bit bigger. Sarah has grown and prospered and she now has two highly successful companies, drives a luxury convertible, owns two investment properties and lives in a beautiful apartment on the water. She now regularly makes $500 000 decisions without blinking an eye. But not one of these is as difficult as taking that first step to borrow some furniture and start to play a bigger game.

There are so many people like Sarah who think that where they are is where they will be forever and that achieving more, being more, doing more and having more is simply not possible. Yet, when you start the process, and continually step up, who knows where you might end up.

Chapter 3 summary

- 👍 You are absolutely awesome.

- 👍 Create more awesome moments than average moments.

- 👍 Awesome moments make your blood pump and your skin tingle.

- 👍 The greatest waste in the world is the waste of human potential.

- 👍 When you get better, the game gets bigger.

MY GAME PLAN:

....

....

....

....

....

....

....

....

....

....

....

....

....

....

....

....

....

....

....

....

....

....

....

....

....

....

....

....

....

....

....

Change is a good thing

Obviously if you want to achieve more, be more, do more and have more, you are going to have to make some changes. I know, scary stuff huh? We hate change, and the reason we hate it so much is that, under the spell of the cotton wool society, we are conditioned to seek out that safe haven where nothing changes, where you can sit safe and sound inside your little cocoon. It's the place where habits form and each day mirrors the last, where we have a conniption if the 6.47 am bus to the city doesn't arrive at 7.03 am, 16 minutes late as usual, or if that skim latte decaf with no sugar actually comes with, oh no, sugar! We live a life of same old, same old, and before we know it we have become old.

Change is not hard. In fact, it's quite simple.

Change! There you go, I said it again, but before you run away and hide under the bed till the storm passes, let me tell you this: change is not hard. Let me say that again, only louder in case you're still under the bed. *Change is not hard!*

In fact, it's quite simple and I am going to show you how not only to do it but to embrace it, make it and live it. I am going to turn you into a lean mean change machine. And guess what: you are going to love it!

The next couple of chapters are your designated change drivers. They will take you on the change journey. They will show you all the sights, tips and tricks for creating and embracing change, and deposit you safely back home. So settle into your seat and get ready to start the change journey. Get ready to find the triggers to your new future, where the games are bigger, better and far more fun than what you are experiencing now.

> You cannot change what has happened, but you have complete control over what happens next!

Three laws of reality

First things first. Let's give ourselves a good, honest reality check. If you want to play a bigger game, you need to embrace the three laws of reality about your life.

Law 1: get real about how things really are

How would you describe your life right now? How is it exactly, truthfully and honestly? Is it everything you really want it to be or are there a few cracks here and there that you are pretending not to notice or trying to cover up so no-one else can see them? If it's a little ordinary or quite average, be honest with yourself about that. You can't go on pretending any more that life is better than it is. If you're in that pretend state of mind you're not going to move onto the path of awesome and play a bigger game. It's no good pretending things are great when they're not. We cannot improve things if we fail to acknowledge how they truly are.

Law 2: get real about how you want life to be

How would you describe your future? Let's get real about the possibilities and making them happen. Let's look at the opportunities that exist and start tapping into them. It's time to be bold and brave about what you really want your life to look like. Create a *really* clear picture of exactly what you want it to be and what you want from it. If life was absolutely awesome, what would be happening, how would you feel, who would you be with, what would you be doing? What is your best possible life? If you can picture the future in your mind, you can make it real.

Law 3: get real about making what you truly want real

How can you make it happen? In the rest of this book I am going to give you all the tools and strategies you'll need to make what you truly want *real*. If you are determined to make it real, whatever you want to achieve, be, do or have can become a reality. But you are going to have to get 'fair dinkum' about making the adjustments, taking the steps and pushing yourself towards achieving something better for yourself. This means making a huge effort. Make a note: no-one else is going to do it for you. Others may well cheer you on and give you a pat on the back now and then, but just as many will pull you down. You and you alone are responsible for what you are and what you become.

You and you alone are responsible for what **you** are and what **you** become.

Clear out the clutter

Now let's clear out some of the clutter that is stopping you from playing a bigger game. It's time to get rid of some of the rubbish you have been carrying around for years that is no longer useful.

You arrived in this world, pure and wonderful, innocent and sweet, full of potential, in a world full of endless opportunities. Somewhere along the way you've become weighed down by a heap of baggage that holds you back, causing you to behave in ways that even you probably don't like.

Before we can hope to achieve more, raise the bar or set higher standards and targets, we need to unload some of this unnecessary baggage from our lives. Let's get rid of the barriers and obstacles that hold us back, the things that get in our way, that cause us stress, frustration and anxiety.

Let's get rid of the **barriers** and **obstacles** that hold us back.

Let's remove all the things that sidetrack and distract us so we can get on the fast track to achieving more than we ever thought possible as we play a bigger game.

Make a list of all the great things you have in your life. List all the things you are proud of—all your achievements, big or small, all the wins and successes. Keep this list and add to it whenever you reach another milestone.

Now create another list—of all the things you have done that you are ashamed of or embarrassed about, the things that, if you had your time again, you would undo, the failures, the stuff-ups and the mega mistakes. Write down the labels you have been given as a result of these actions.

Now take that list, fold it in half. Hold it in both hands, close your eyes and concentrate on what you have written. Now tear that paper into little pieces and throw it in the bin.

You are not your past. You cannot drive down a freeway looking in the rear-view mirror. The reason the windscreen is so big is so you can see clearly what's in front of you. The rear-view mirror is small and used only briefly to check what's behind you.

You have just got rid of everything in your rear-view mirror. You are not your past, no matter how bad or how ugly it may seem. You have no influence over your past, only over your future.

Having emptied your backpack of all that unwanted rubbish, you can now fill it with all the exciting changes you want to make for your future.

In a heartbeat

Do you know how quickly you can change your future? In a heartbeat, just like that. There will be a moment, and it might be today, when that heartbeat, that boom hits and you decide:

- 👍 I'm going to change my life.
- 👍 I'm going to change my direction.
- 👍 I'm going to change where I go and what I do.
- 👍 I'm going to change how I behave.
- 👍 I'm going to change what I do at work.
- 👍 I'm going to be more committed to my relationships.
- 👍 I'm going to be better with my friends.
- 👍 I'm going to be more careful with my finances.
- 👍 I'm going to be more committed to achieving the things I want to achieve.

In a heartbeat—boom, boom!

A **heartbeat** is all it takes to make that one decision that will reshape your **life** forever.

It's that quick. I have seen people give up smoking on the spot. In a heartbeat. In the past I have seen people instantly resolve to give rather than take in their relationships, in a heartbeat. I have seen people go from hating their job to giving their absolute best in everything they do, in a heartbeat. And I have seen people go from spending every cent they had, and everyone else's, to creating a solid financial platform, yes, you guessed it—in a heartbeat.

A heartbeat is all it takes to make that one decision that will reshape your life forever, to resolve to play a bigger game. No matter what!

Pete—stepping up a level

Pete is a great friend of mine. For years he had been slowly developing his business and getting some great results. A few years ago he had settled into a rhythm and a pattern that was quite comfortable. Business was easy and the money was good. One day we were having a chat and he admitted he was getting bored. I suggested maybe he should step it up a level. He said he was at the top of his game—there was no more he could do.

Here is the danger: when you get that comfortable, when it's easy and you are just going through the motions—that's when you are on the edge of a decline or, worse, you could already be on the way down.

I suggested to Pete that something had to change or he was going to pay a price. He knew I was serious, so he gave it some thought and talked with his family. Then he made a massive change. He sold his business, packed his family up and moved to another town in another state, and he started again from scratch.

The result? A new lease on life, a new and more successful business and business model, a new group of friends and colleagues, and a new direction that has stretched him to achieve new things.

Twelve months after the change I asked him, 'Was the change a good thing?' He replied, 'It has been fantastic! I just didn't realise what I was capable of. I had become comfortable and stale and that had started to find its way into my personal life and relationships. I needed the change, badly.'

Chapter 4 summary

- 👍 You are going to have to make some changes.
- 👍 Change is not hard; in fact, it's quite simple.
- 👍 The three laws of reality are:
    - Get real about how things really are.
    - Get real about how you really want things to be.
    - Get real about making these things real.
- 👍 Clear out the clutter that's stopping you from playing a bigger game.
- 👍 Remove all the things that distract and sidetrack you.
- 👍 You can change your life in a heartbeat.

MY GAME PLAN:

....

....

....

....

....

....

....

....

....

....

....

....

....

....

....

....

....

....

....

....

....

....

....

....

....

....

....

....

....

....

....

....

Play to your
potential

Live every day as if it is your last, because one day it will be!

In this chapter, we will focus on just how much potential you really have. This will help you make the most of all future opportunities and ensure that you never waste another minute. Most of us follow a similar pattern through life. We step through one stage after another in a fairly predictable sequence. Falling into this pattern does not necessarily allow us to reach our potential and get the most out of everything we do.

> **Live** every day as if it's your last, because **one day** it will be.

The model shown in figure 5.1, overleaf, which tracks *potential* versus *time*, will help us visualise these patterns and how they affect us. Line A on the graph represents the predictable pattern we follow. We are born, learn to walk, feed ourselves, ride a bike and turn a cartwheel. We are then sent off to school, where we learn mathematics, English, sports and drama. We leave school, get a job, buy a car, find a partner and settle down. Before we know it we have kids, a mortgage and credit card debt, and we are so busy we struggle to fit everything in.

At this point we start to put things off: I'll take that holiday when the kids are a bit older. I'll start that new business once the mortgage is settled. I'll learn another language when the kids leave school. We'll go on that big adventure after the kids leave home. This is what some people describe as a mid-life crisis, my definition of which is 'having more life to live than you have life left'.

Figure 5.1: potential versus time

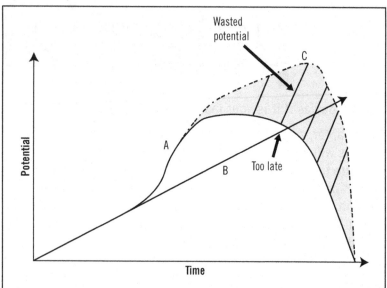

Before you know it you are old. You have left your run too late. The to-do list is a mile long and you start to give up on some of your dreams. You convince yourself that you are too old and there are things that an old person just can't do.

Line B in figure 5.1 represents time. This is how time moves: it is constant and keeps ticking by, waiting for no-one. The point where it passes through potential is the point where you have lost an opportunity, because your potential is on the decline (line A)

In the model, if you haven't realised all your potential when the time line passes through the potential line, you're already on the decline, on the way out. It's too late to achieve what you have always wanted. Many people choose this average life path. Do you want to live your life like that? Is it what you want for yourself?

It doesn't have to be like that. As I have already told you, life is a wonderful adventure and I truly believe that you can live it to the max, squeezing every drop out of it, right to the very end.

That's what I mean to do. I intend not only to follow my dreams but to live them fully, to realise my hopes and dreams and get *all* the things done that I ever wanted (that's line C in figure 5.1). I want to die still living life to the max. I don't want to slide out of existence after retiring with a soft, gentle sigh. I want to go out with a bang and a shout, screaming at the top of my lungs, *woohoo*, what a ride!

I want to go out with a **bang** and a **shout**, screaming at the top of my lungs *woohoo*, what a ride!

One of the major problems for all of us is that we believe the game of life goes on forever or at least for a long, long time. We imagine that we are going to live to a hundred and get that letter from the queen. We think we have so much time left that we can always leave playing a bigger game till tomorrow, or the next day, or maybe next week, next month or next year...We persuade ourselves:

- 👍 I can do that later.
- 👍 I've got another year.
- 👍 What's the rush?
- 👍 Next year I'll run that marathon.
- 👍 I can lose the weight later.
- 👍 I'll go on that holiday next year.

And while people are floating along, they are slowly letting opportunities pass until they reach that stage in life when they say:

- 👍 I wouldn't be able to do it now.
- 👍 I'm getting too old — it's not going to happen.
- 👍 It's not going to work out.

If the game of **life** was only going to last one week, how hard would you **play**?

Most of us have played a team sport. Imagine if that game went on forever. If you are playing basketball you have to pace yourself a little bit. 'I'm not going to go too hard because I don't want to wear myself out.' But if you knew the game had only 10 minutes to go and you had a good chance of winning, how hard would you play? Flat out! Wouldn't you? You know what? The game of life doesn't go on forever.

This was a really big revelation for me. I used to live my life thinking the game goes on forever. Then I got some real-life lessons on just how short life can be.

Play like there is no tomorrow, because one day there won't be one.

When I was 19, my best mate and I travelled around Australia for 12 months on our motorbikes. We camped in a little three-man tent, picking up odd jobs here and there, going from one adventure and one party to the next. It was an awesome, awesome trip. A few months after we got back, he was travelling home to the Snowy Mountains. It was just before Christmas. He was hit by a car driven by a drunk driver and was killed.

Then I had another wake-up call. Most blokes only ever really have one true best mate. It's a little different for women as they seem to be able to manage multiple best friends, but for us guys, there's usually only one best mate. And if you lose him, the chances of finding another one are pretty slim.

I was lucky. When I moved to the Gold Coast to play football I connected with another bloke and we became best mates. So we hung out and did all the things that best mates do, enjoying life to the max, oblivious to whatever was happening in the rest of the world. He appeared to be one of the most down-to-earth and contented guys I ever knew, but then, for a reason no-one could understand, he took his own life.

It was another harsh reminder that life can be too short and that I probably needed to play the game a bit harder now.

Some people say things happen in threes, and it was the third instance of someone close to me passing away that gave me the real wake-up call. I had an older brother and I was always saying I must go and see him. I must spend more time with him and his family, get to know them all better. Then one day I received a phone call to say my older brother had passed away. He'd had a heart attack at the ripe old age of 50. I went to the funeral and was given the opportunity to see his body. As I entered the room, I saw him in the coffin. He was dressed in his favourite shirt and he looked alive. I walked over and kissed him on the forehead, and then it hit me: he's not here, it's too late. I had missed so many opportunities to share my life with him and let him share his life with me.

Finally it really hit me that the game of life does not go on forever. You get one shot at it and there is no time to be miserable or to accept second best. The opportunity is there every day to have an awesome experience and play a bigger game. You're an awesome individual and you can achieve so many things if you just step up into that place.

You get one **shot** at life and there is no time to be miserable or accept second **best**.

You have so much potential and endless opportunity. You are capable of so much. I am going to tell you some of my success stories throughout this book to illustrate how I have gathered up potential in both arms and used it to achieve some remarkable results. I'm not telling you these stories to impress you but to impress on you that success leaves clues. There are many, many people who have achieved remarkable results and will happily share with you the clues to those successes. There are also people out there who will tell you to stay back and not do this, don't give a try, it won't work. Don't listen to them. You have massive potential. It is my hope that in telling you the stories about my successes you will find some clues to achieving your own.

Success leaves clues.

After all, I am an average guy from an average town who grew up in an average family. I had a very average attitude, but when the bombshell finally hit home I was able to choose to play a bigger game every day. There are people who have less than you but achieve more than you, and there are people with far more than you achieving less than you. It does not matter where you come from, where you have been or what you have.

Potential lies within us all. The secret of **success** is to unleash it.

Potential lies within all of us. The secret of success is to unleash it. Unfortunately, potential cannot be banked. What you don't use now is gone forever. Potential is useful only if you choose to apply it.

Zac — the grass is not always greener

Zac came to one of my events a few years ago. I got the opportunity to speak with him briefly before the event and asked him what it was he was looking to get out of the day. His reply was, 'I want a change. I want to get the confidence to make a change. I have been an accountant for 37 years and I hate it. I want to change and I want it badly'. I told him to focus on that and to see what the forum delivered.

This event drew more than 500 people and in such a context it is impossible to concentrate on a single individual's needs. The reality is we are all looking for the motivation, inspiration and perhaps the agitation that will bring about change. I knew there would be heaps of great ideas that Zac could use to make the change. He just needed to want it badly enough to take action.

About 10 weeks later I was down at the beach watching the sunrise at my favourite spot when to my surprise Zac showed up! Apparently I had let it slip that I watched the sunrise pretty much every day when I was in town and he knew which town I was in.

The biggest surprise was that Zac was still an accountant, but it seemed he was now a very, very happy accountant. When I asked him what had changed, Zac explained that I had helped him see that while he needed a change, he also needed to include things he loved in his life. Turns out Zac loved doing people's accounts, he just didn't love the admin — invoicing, filing and so on. So he arranged for someone who did love the admin to do that part of his job so he could concentrate on the parts he loved. Sometimes it's not radical change we need but a simple adjustment to our existing circumstances. For Zac, moving to another accounting firm would probably just have produced the same result.

Playing a bigger game in his own backyard brought Zac a lot of happiness.

Chapter 5 summary

- Live every day as if it is your last, because one day it will be.

- When the time line passes through the potential line, it's too late.

- Go out with a bang and a shout, screaming at the top of your lungs, *woohoo*, what a ride!

- The game of life is short. Play hard.

- You have so much potential; you have so much opportunity; you are capable of so much.

MY GAME PLAN:

....

....

....

....

....

....

You *can* do it

I have had some really amazing, awesome experiences in my life because I have been able to say 'I can' where most people say 'I can't'. I have been able to continue on when others give up; I have been able to get back up when I fall over; to keep going when others are worn out. I like to refer to this as determination, although there are people who describe me as stubborn. It doesn't really matter how you describe it, the reality is that I believe *I can*, and that makes a massive difference. You might be thinking, well, how do you get to that point of belief, Rowdy? How do you get to the point where you decide, 'Yes I *can*', rather than 'No I *can't*'?

You get there by answering two questions. The first is 'Can I do it?' Could little old me possibly take on something like that? The second is 'Will it be worth it?' Are the potential benefits of trying something new going to be great enough for the effort involved?

To answer the first question you need to consider two more: First, do I have the capability? No skills probably equals no chance unless you are prepared to go and learn those skills, practising until you have developed them. Second, do I have the confidence? Do I trust or believe in myself enough to give it a go?

No skills probably equals no chance.

An example of combining my capability and my confidence was my decision to run a marathon. I read somewhere that less than 1 per cent of the population have ever run a full marathon.

When I first read that statistic, I thought that's me, I want to be in that 1 per cent. At the time I wasn't particularly fit, I wasn't a great runner but I thought this would be a really cool thing to do. So with a little bit of confidence and a touch of capability I booked myself in for the Gold Coast Marathon. I prepared for it and I turned up.

To run a marathon you must turn up at about 5.00 am, unless you're really anxious and turn up at 4.00 am, as I did. It's cold and dark and scary. Lots of intense people, a strange environment and unusual circumstances, at least for a beginner like me.

Playing a bigger game can be like that. It can be a bit scary. You're going to find yourself in an environment that you've never been in before. You will find yourself in unusual or uncomfortable circumstances. You're going to step into a place outside that cotton wool society. But trust me, you can do it. Playing a bigger game is not as hard as you think.

When you run a marathon they put you in a starting time based on where you anticipate finishing. I was in the three- to four-hour bracket. I remember standing there wondering how this was all going to work out.

Then I started to make critical mistakes, I began to make comparisons. I looked over at a guy near me, he wore the best running shoes I'd ever seen. They looked like they cost $1000. He had the best shorts, the right t-shirt; he had all the gear. He even had mittens and a beanie on to keep in the heat. He looked like he was going fast just standing on the spot.

I was standing there wondering, 'Geez Rowdy, have you prepared enough? Have you done enough for this?' I looked a bit further over and saw a girl who looked so fit and so sharp you could see her muscles rippling. I was thinking, 'Am I in the right group? Have I chosen the right place? Am I going to make it?'

And I remember looking over at the guy beside me, who was 20 kilos heavier than I was, thinking, 'Buddy, you should go to the back.' We do that, don't we? We make comparisons; we're sometimes very quick to make comparisons. And when we get caught up in comparisons, sometimes we make excuses and say to ourselves, 'I'm going to stay in my cotton wool because it's scary out there.' That's what I was doing.

It's easy to convince yourself that you're not good enough, tough enough, strong enough, that you have not prepared enough. But the key is to begin. Just start and see what unfolds.

The good thing about the marathon is that when the gun goes off you have to begin or get run over by the thousands of people behind you. No backing out now. So off I went and I found a bit of a rhythm. I was going really well and meeting all my time targets. I had my times written down my arm and I was tracking myself and I was going really well, slightly ahead of my scheduled times. Then I decided to raise the bar, to step it up a notch. I chose another runner in the distance and decided he would be my next target.

So I focused on catching this guy and started running him down. Every kilometre I would gain about 100 metres on him. I was getting closer all the time, and when I was just behind him I started to stick my chest out and get my arms going because I really wanted to overtake him looking like it was the easiest thing in the world to do. I was almost level with him.

> The satisfaction of success, lasts long after the pain of playing all in!

In a marathon they have water stations at 5 km intervals, and he chose that moment to pull up at the water station like it was the best bar in town. This was when the mental barrier kicked in.

There I was all pumped, ready to overtake this guy and he pulled into that water station and started drinking water like it was tequila. My conscience, that annoying voice in your head that threatens to undermine your goals, tempted me to change my plans. 'You know what, Rowdy, why don't you join the guy? Take a break? You can catch the time up later on, it doesn't matter. You need a drink, and in fact you need a bit of a rest. Why don't you just lie down on the grass and watch the world go by? You can run a marathon next year.'

You will have this experience if you choose to play a bigger game. You'll come up against the mental barriers, tempting you to cop out and throw in the towel, coaxing you back into the old cotton wool society. It is a challenge that you need to push through. This is where most people struggle and fail. They give up in their head before they have built up momentum, before they start to see some results. This is when you need the determination and discipline to continue where others give up. Fortunately I got through that, left the guy and the drink stand behind and ran on.

I got to the halfway mark of that marathon at Burleigh Heads and got a great surprise: my family was at the turning point to cheer me on. My four-year-old son, Joshua, ran with me for about 200 metres, and it nearly killed him. Do you think it made a difference to me? Absolutely. I remember looking at a bloke beside me who looked like he was going to collapse and thinking that two kilometres back I had felt just like him.

You'll have this experience when you choose to play a bigger game. You'll have family, friends, partners and colleagues who give you a boost, a tap on the shoulder and a helping hand along the way. These people help put a smile back on your face when it gets a bit tough. They encourage you to continue your journey and pursue your dreams.

I will never forget the boost Josh gave me by running those 200 metres; it encouraged me to keep on, to continue even though I was exhausted, lifting me just when I was beginning to struggle.

Five kilometres later the toenail on my left big toe came off completely and my shoe filled with blood. At that point the physical barriers set in. I was squishing along—squish, pace, squish, pace. I thought to myself, 'This is too much pain, this is too hard. I'm going to throw the towel in. I don't want to run any more.'

Just like the mental barriers, the physical barriers will make you want to give up. This is what average people do. They experience physical barriers and they just want to call it quits. But nothing worth having comes easy. I decided to keep going just a little bit longer. I thought if I could just squish along for another 100 metres and then see how it was, then 100 metres more and then another 100 metres more and after a while the pain was gone.

You too will face physical challenges on the journey to playing a bigger game. You will need to be out there trying things, practising things, doing new things. You will lose energy. You will struggle with your confidence. People will be trying to hold you back. Trying to get you to do things the way average people do them. You'll be tired and you'll be worn out but you will need to push through that. Most people give up the struggle just before success arrives. Sometimes you just have to keep at it, keep going and then all of a sudden stuff starts to happen.

I was worn out and I pushed through that. I got to the 40-kilometre mark in the marathon. Now, anyone who has run a marathon will tell you that when you get to the 40-kilometre mark, you are pumped because you know that even if you have to crawl the rest of the way you're going to make it. You get this feeling of exhilaration and excitement.

The race of **life** is long and in the end it's really only with **yourself**.

So I got to the 40-kilometre mark and was going really well. I was feeling great! I knew I was going to finish and was elated. At that point a guy in a gorilla suit went past me. Then just to top it off that guy who was 20 kilos heavier than me, went past. You know what? I didn't care. I didn't care because I'd learned something very important in that 40 kilometres, I'd learned that the race of life is long and in the end it's really only with yourself. It's the struggle with yourself to achieve more, be more, do more and have more that's important. No-one but you can make you a better person.

I thought about why I'd decided to run the marathon. Initially, I went on that journey because I wanted to be in that 1 per cent who had done it. I wanted the photo, the medal and the T-shirt. What I got was something completely different. If you go on the journey of the bigger game, if you choose today to step out of the cotton wool society, to get off the loop of the average and move onto the path of the awesome, you may have some idea of the things you want to achieve. But like me I am sure you will find that the rewards will be far greater than those you initially imagined.

After I crossed the finish line in a time of 3 hours 34 minutes, I got the medal, the T-shirt and the finishing photo I'd wanted. I also won the confidence to push through the boundaries, challenge myself and get out of my comfort zone, and the understanding that I could play a bigger game. Most important, though, it had given me a wonderful experience as a father. The 200 metres I shared with Josh were probably one of the best things I have ever done with him. The photo of the two of us running the marathon sits on my desk and inspires me every single day of my life.

So I embarked on this journey for one set of reasons and came out with a whole set of unexpected outcomes. I came out with something that provides me with a daily inspiration. I also learned that three and a half hours in a marathon is not that big a drama. Before you do it, it seems like it's enormous but once you've done it, it's no big deal.

Look for **opportunities** to play a bigger game, to put yourself in the **top 1 per cent**.

Anyone can run a marathon, I promise you. It's not that hard. You just need to have some running ability, develop some confidence, match it with a little discipline and determination and you are on your way. And this applies to any other way you may choose to play a bigger game. Get yourself ready, do the preparation, turn up, push through the mental and physical barriers, and you can do it.

If you apply this to the rest of your life you can be awesome at whatever it is you desire. But if you're caught up in the cotton wool society, you will be plagued with doubts and reservations. So let's deal with those.

Let's look at how you can get from *can't* to *can*. The can/can't matrix in figure 6.1, overleaf, takes account of capability and confidence to measure the potential to succeed with specific goals.

Figure 6.1: the can/can't matrix

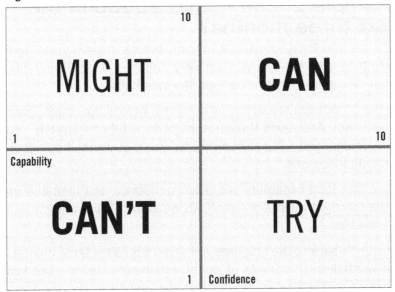

The capability axis is horizontal and ranges from 1 through to 10. The confidence axis is vertical and ranges from 1 through to 10. You can use this model to ask yourself any question.

Example 1: am I good enough to apply for that promotion?

Measure yourself on the capability axis first. Can you do all that the job requires of you? How capable are you on a scale of 1 to 10 (1 being *Not at all capable*, 5 being *Reasonably capable* and 10 being *Very capable*)?

Let's say you are feeling 7 out of 10 on the capability axis. Next measure how confident you feel about applying for the promotion. Let's say you are feeling 3 out of 10 on the confidence axis. If you plot the 7 on the horizontal axis and the 3 on the vertical axis, you end up in the TRY quadrant.

This means you should try for the position, but unless you work on your confidence before you go for the interview it is highly likely you will sabotage the opportunity.

Example 2: can I save $5000 in the next three months?

Let's say you have saved that amount before, have regular work coming in and believe you are very capable of achieving this target. You plot yourself as a 9 on the capability axis.

On the confidence scale, having done this before, your confidence is also high. And, even though it might be a bit of a stretch, you are confident you will achieve this. So you plot yourself as a 9 on the confidence axis.

If you plot 9 on capability and 9 on confidence, you then end up in the top right quadrant—the CAN quadrant. You know you will achieve that.

Let's think back to the first time you saved $5000 in three months. You went through periods of doubt, challenges, fears—but you achieved it. Most tasks are difficult the first time, but the more we do it the better we become. The more capable we become, the more confident we are.

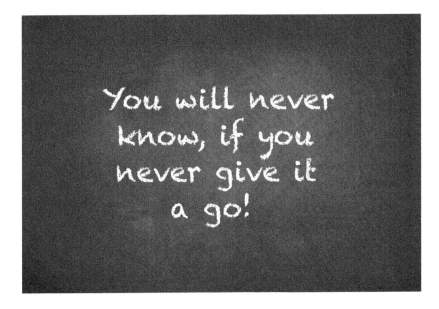

The can/can't matrix is a fantastic model to use regularly when faced with decisions as you move from the average path to the awesome path and beyond to playing a much bigger game.

Strategies for dealing with the results of the can/can't matrix

Decision making is much simpler once you have checked the results of the can/can't matrix test.

Can

If your result lands in the CAN quadrant, get on with it. Create an execution plan and get the ball rolling. You can do it. You have the skills and the confidence to get the job done. Be aware, though, that sometimes when we get a result in the CAN box it's because our goal is not big enough. We haven't stretched or challenged ourselves enough.

If your result is comfortably inside the CAN box, then I would suggest you need to make your goal a little more challenging, otherwise you are in danger of falling into the comfort zone.

Try

If your result lands in the TRY box, then you may attempt your goal, but it is likely you will fail. You have the confidence to give it a go, but a lack of skills may hold you back.

Make a list of the skills you will need to complete your goal, tick the ones you are strong in and put a cross against the ones where you have a weakness. Now go to work on your weaknesses, either by developing the skills required or by finding a way to get around them.

Might

When your result lands in the MIGHT box it means that you have the required skills and abilities to complete the task but that you may not complete it well because you lack the confidence to follow through. If this is the case for you, then consider breaking down the task or goal into smaller steps. This allows you to experience small wins that will give you confidence. Stack these small wins on top of each other and you start to gain some momentum, which in turn builds confidence.

Can't

CAN'T is the really difficult place to start from when pursuing a goal. Do not despair, however, as it is still possible to achieve your desired result. To make your goal a reality you are going to need two additional things on top of the strategies in the TRY and MIGHT sections. First, you will need *determination*. You can get from *can't* to *can* but you have to really, really want it. You need an 'all or nothing', 'whatever it takes' mentality that means you just will not give up. The other thing you will need is *discipline*—the ability to set a course of action and never to waiver from it, to stick to your plans no matter what shows up.

I faced these challenges in running my marathon. You too will experience marathon-like challenges and you will have to dig deep, plot your capability and confidence on the matrix, and, most of all, start believing in yourself.

If you don't **believe** in you, how can anyone else **believe** in you?

At the beginning of this chapter I explained that there were two questions we need to ask ourselves. The first was 'Can I do it?' The second was 'Will it be worth it?' In the previous section we answered the first question. Now it's time to address the second. The next model, the risk versus reward matrix in figure 6.2, will help us decide whether the benefits are worth the risks.

Figure 6.2: the risk versus reward matrix

In this matrix the reward axis is horizontal (left to right) and ranges from Low (1) on the left to High (10) on the right. The risk axis is vertical (top to bottom) and ranges from Low (1) at the top to High (10) at the bottom. Note that High is at the bottom of this axis.

You can use this model to ask yourself any question in relation to whether or not taking on a challenge will be 'worth it'.

Let's use the same examples as we used in the can/can't matrix in figure 6.1.

Example 1: am I good enough to apply for that promotion?

First, measure yourself on the reward axis (left to right). Will the benefit of the promotion be worth the risks associated with the position? How great will the benefit be for you on a scale of 1 to 10 (1 representing *Not at all rewarding*, 5 being *Reasonably rewarding* and 10 indicating *Highly rewarding*)? Let's say you opt for 7 out of 10 on the reward axis.

Next measure the risks in applying for the promotion. You might think of the risks in terms of job security, extra hours and impact on your personal life. Let's say you are feeling about a 3 out of 10 on the risk axis (top to bottom). Remember that High is at the bottom, so a 3 is a fairly low risk.

If you plot the 7 on the horizontal axis and the 3 on the vertical axis, you end up in the YES quadrant. This means the potentially high rewards and relatively low risks indicate you should definitely push hard for the position, giving it your best shot.

Example 2: can I save $5000 in the next three months?

You have experienced the rewards of saving that amount before (a fantastic holiday!), so you know the benefits of having $5000 in the bank. You plot it as a 9 on the reward axis.

You know also that saving that amount of money means you have to completely give up your social life. You don't get to hang out with your friends and meet new people. You don't have a boyfriend/girlfriend or partner and time is ticking by; you'd like to settle down in the not too distant future. So you plot this as a 9 on the risk axis, which is near the bottom, therefore a very high risk.

So if we plot 9 on reward and 9 on risk, you then end up in the bottom-right MAYBE quadrant. This result suggests that perhaps you should reconsider your goal, as the task may cause you some anxiety and stress. Either aim for a slightly less challenging target or choose to focus on something else.

The risk versus reward matrix is a great tool for helping you decide whether a challenge is worth taking up—that is, the pay-off of playing a bigger game.

Yes

If your result was in the YES quadrant, the pay-off will definitely be worth it and it really is a no-brainer. Low risk combined with high reward means you should be very satisfied with the outcome.

Maybe

If your result was in this box, then the rewards are great but they come at a fairly high risk. You should weigh up the options carefully, see if you can find any ways to lower the risks or avoid them completely. Sometimes high reward/high risk scenarios are worth pursuing, and they most definitely stretch you, but you should also be aware that they can end in disaster.

Unlikely

When your results land in this quadrant the risks are quite low, but so are the rewards. So the challenge may not be highly rewarding but it is often the source of a quick, easy win.

No

If you land in this box you have got to be aware that the chances of success are not great, mainly because you have staked a lot for very little return. It's best to avoid a scenario that ends up in this quadrant. Look for alternatives. If you do decide to go ahead, then look for ways to increase the pay-off and lower the risks associated with the challenge.

Danielle — a story with a great ending

I once ran an executive retreat for a company over a weekend. The aim was to focus on helping the company play a bigger game. Part of the process is helping individuals in a team to play a bigger game in life and at work.

There were 24 executives at the retreat. They did not know much about what was going to happen, other than that it was to be inspiring, motivational and challenging. Danielle was part of the team. Of the 24 participants she seemed the most distracted and disconnected from the rest of the group. In fact, she was the only one who just didn't seem to want to be there, showing no enthusiasm, interest or energy. So I made it my job to see if I could turn that around.

Sometimes we get so caught up in the present or, even worse, the past that we cannot see the possibilities that exist in the future. We find playing the current game so difficult that the idea of playing bigger just seems inconceivable.

With Danielle, her answer to every possibility was 'can't', so over the next two days we worked on getting to 'can', finding the confidence and capability to be able to say 'Yes I can' or 'Yes I will'.

When Danielle left with the rest of the team on Sunday she was excited about the possibilities, both for the company and for herself.

Three months later I got a surprise call from Danielle inviting me to her wedding, and she asked if we could get together for a coffee so she could explain why she wanted me to come. When we met for coffee the following week she explained that before the retreat she had given up on life. She'd had enough. In fact, she had written a suicide note the previous week and fully intended to take her own life. She decided the retreat would be her last chance. If she couldn't find some meaning in her life there, then that week would be her last.

She wanted me to come to her wedding because on that weekend we had worked through the 'can't /can' model and she had found the ability to believe in herself, to play a bigger game. She had reunited with her boyfriend and found a passion for life again.

Danielle can; you can; we all can play a bigger game. We just need to draw a line in the sand where we are now and step across it to start the journey.

Chapter 6 summary

🖒 There are two questions we must answer.

   – Can I do it?

   – Will it be worth it?

🖒 High capability + confidence = CAN.

🖒 High rewards + low risk = WORTH IT.

🖒 Choose to be in the top 1 per cent.

🖒 Get yourself ready, do the preparation, turn up and do it!

🖒 If you don't believe in you, how can anyone else believe in you?

MY GAME PLAN:

....

....

....

....

....

....

....

....

....

....

....

....

....

....

....

Chapter 7
Stretch the boundaries

Now it's time to really step up to the plate, take some action and get outside your comfort zone. Our comfort zone is the zone where nothing happens. It's the place where we grow fat and old, the place where goals, dreams, ideas and ambitions fade into oblivion.

Top achievers have an ever-expanding comfort zone. They develop and grow, learn new things, have new experiences open broader horizons. Expanding your comfort zone develops confidence and allows you to make the impossible possible.

Let's examine the zones individually from the model in figure 7.1.

Figure 7.1: the zones of experience

Comfort zone

That's the little warm and fuzzy place we stay, where it's nice and safe and we don't get hurt. We're wrapped in cotton wool and it really doesn't matter what we do because nothing can possibly harm us. We always feel safe in our comfort zone, but unfortunately we can't possibly grow from there.

Learning/ability zone

The next zone outside our comfort zone is called our learning zone. How do you get out of your comfort zone and into your learning zone? It's easy — just start taking little steps, little nudges, little pushes. Start trying things you have never done before. Challenge yourself a little bit. Think of the things you do now that are easy and step them up a level. The way to get out of our comfort zone is to push gradually against the boundaries and as we do we learn we are more capable than we thought.

How long is it since you tried something for the first time? Why not try something different every day, until your comfort level expands and you move deeper into the learning zone? At first it may be scary. It's a little like learning to drive. Initially you are all over the road, you crunch through the gears, forget the indicators, stall at the traffic lights and tremble in your shoes every time a semi-trailer whips past your side mirror. As you gain more confidence, experience and courage, you handle the car more professionally, until eventually you get your licence and before you know it driving is a breeze.

The other name I give this zone is our *ability zone*. To read this book is to step into your ability zone. Some readers by now will have already made choices and decisions about things they are going to do that are outside the cotton wool society. By making the decision to act on what they learn from this book they have already pushed themselves into their learning zone.

Fear zone

Outside our learning zone, we come to the fear zone. Mainly because it's a couple of zones away from our comfy little cotton wool society, where we are all wrapped up and protected from harm, the fear zone is a really scary place to go. We put things in this zone that we are unlikely to do unless we are pushed to the limit, as in an emergency or life-threatening situation.

Impossible zone

Beyond the fear zone is the impossible zone. This is where we push all those things that are never going to happen—the things we could never imagine doing under any circumstances. Public speaking is one example (some people are more afraid of public speaking than they are of dying). Others are making a million dollars, having the freedom that comes with owning a successful business, being the CEO of a multimillion-dollar company or running a marathon. These were all things that once existed in my impossible zone but are now well and truly in my comfort zone.

Take a few minutes to create a list of the things that are in each of your zones. What do you do with absolute ease, without even thinking? This is your comfort zone. What would stretch you a bit—what could you do that you would find a little challenging but with some effort you could do it? This is your learning zone. What about the things you would like to do but scare the pants off you but you might just do if you really had to? This is your fear zone. And finally, what are the things you would dearly love to do but just cannot imagine any way they could happen? This is your impossible zone.

Making the impossible possible

So how do we make the impossible possible? It's quite easy actually. When we expand our comfort zone into our learning zone by pushing the boundaries, stretching and challenging ourselves, we create new levels of skill and confidence, and this becomes our new, broader comfort zone. Now what was once our fear zone becomes our new learning zone. So the things we were once afraid of doing we now just need to learn to do—they have become much easier. What was scary and unlikely is now just something we need to learn how to do.

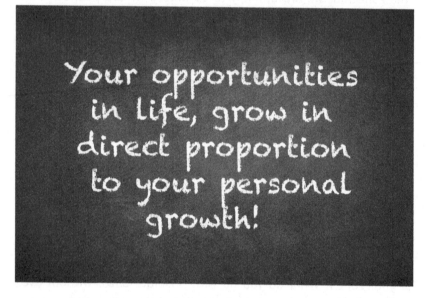

The amazing thing that happens as you grow and develop is that each zone dissolves into the next. The impossible zone has now become the fear zone. This means that the things that you would have imagined would just never happen are now scary but possible. That's how you make the impossible possible.

Top **achievers** have an ever-expanding **comfort** zone.

So making the impossible possible is a simple process. You just need to gradually step into that space and look for those little challenges, building the little success stories and confidence boosts that are going to take you on that journey. Or you can sit back, wrap yourself up in cotton wool and watch life go by and, like Brendan, hope that luck turns up for you.

When you grab life by the scruff of the neck and say, 'I don't want to be caught up in this cotton wool society any more; I want to step up to the plate and do something really awesome; I'm going to push my learning zone, stretch out into my fear zone and make the impossible possible', you will notice the change!

One of the ways we do this is by creating new ways of doing things. The easiest way to change your life or to change your circumstances is to change your standards. Are the standards by which you now live good enough to take you where you want to go? Is the peer group you hang out with likely to raise the bar for you? If you're in a peer group that just 'gets by', how are they going to respond every time you try to get out of that zone? They're going to pull you back.

If the peer group I'm in is going to keep me in my comfort zone, then I don't want to stay in it. Is your peer group just going through the motions of life (you know, the guys who turn up at the pub every Friday night to have the same old whinge about the same old things, or the group of girls who go to lunch together and pick everyone apart when they go off to the bathroom)? If this rings true for you, then maybe you need to make a change. Sure, you may lose a few friends along the way, but I have found that your true friends (the winners) are the ones who last the distance and support you in your journey to a bigger game.

It's a good idea, too, to consider who you might be accepting advice from. Who is giving you directions on how to play a bigger game? Maybe it's time to raise the bar on the type of mentors you rely on. I see people out there who take financial advice from someone driving a '72 Commodore. It's a no-brainer, isn't it? If he's so good at finance, why is he driving an old bomb? I see people who take advice from a doctor who is 30 kilos overweight and chain-smokes. That is not the mentor I want giving me advice about my health. I see people who have had three divorces dishing out advice on relationships. Someone who has made a mess of three such important relationships is probably not the person best qualified to advise you on how to make the most of yours. And don't accept career advice from someone who has lost their job time after time.

Look for those little **challenges**, little **success** stories.

One of the other things we can do to get out of our comfort zone and step into that new place is to stretch the boundaries. We can push ourselves and challenge ourselves to create a life that's full of energy, excitement, enthusiasm and challenges that make every day an adventure. The truly exciting part of life lies at the edges of our comfort zone.

So how simple is it to challenge yourself every day? When was the last time you didn't drink coffee for a week? When was the last time you didn't have a block of chocolate for a month? They're the little challenges that say 'I'm tough enough. I'm good enough. I'm strong enough', that may push back through the boundaries that you place around yourself. A friend of mine just turned 50, and every time he turns a decade he gives up alcohol for a year, just to challenge himself, to know he can give it up. It's his way of stretching and testing his boundaries.

How can you challenge yourself? What can you give up or stop doing? What negative or destructive things are going on that you can step out of? Interestingly, another thing you can do to get out of your comfort zone is stop trying to do too much—stop doing 100 things badly and start doing a couple of big things really, really well.

However you go about it, there is no way you can possibly play a bigger game if you are not prepared to move out of your comfort zone.

Janelle — stretching to win

From time to time I have the privilege of mentoring an aspiring speaker, someone who wants either to earn a living by speaking at conferences, meetings and events, or to use speaking as a way to position themselves as an expert in their industry or to market their business.

I don't do a great deal of this type of mentoring because I find that very few people are prepared to do what it takes. Few will stretch themselves hard enough to escape their comfort zone and get the results. Janelle was different. Everything I threw at her she did. Every task I gave her she completed; every idea we developed she tested; every strategy we devised she implemented.

Eventually she asked me if we could run an event and speak on stage together. My typical response to such a request is a resounding *no*, but I decided to give Janelle an opportunity. I said to her, 'You arrange everything—the date, the room, the equipment, the logistics—and put 100 people in a room, and I will turn up and speak for free.' On top of this she would need to put together her own speech and deliver it for the first time on the night. Most people would have found the challenge, let alone the thought of speaking to an audience of 100 people, too big a stretch. (In fact, research has shown that one in four people fear public speaking more than dying!)

Janelle got almost 200 people in a room and stood on stage and did a better job of presenting than I did. She said she was so nervous and so scared, but she was really glad she had stretched herself because now she truly believed she could do what she wanted to do.

Chapter 7 summary

- 👍 Get out of your comfort zone.

- 👍 Stretch your comfort zone into your learning zone.

- 👍 As you stretch one zone into the next, the impossible starts to become possible.

- 👍 The easiest way to change your circumstances is to change your standards.

- 👍 Find a peer group that wants to play a bigger game.

- 👍 Be careful who you accept advice from.

- 👍 Challenge yourself every day.

MY GAME PLAN:

....

....

....

....

....

....

....

....

....

....

....

....

....

....

....

....

....

....

....

....

Five great lies—don't be misled

There are five great lies we live by that stop us from introducing any significant change in our life. These lies, as we'll now see, definitely prevent us from playing a bigger game.

Lie 1: not enough time

How often do you hear someone say, 'I just don't have the time' or 'I will when...' (when I win the lottery, when I get married, when the kids grow up, when I retire, etc.)? You have exactly the same amount of time in your day as did Mozart, Michelangelo, Muhammad Ali, Margaret Thatcher, Mother Teresa, and the list goes on...

Everyone gets **24** hours per day; use every **minute** wisely.

We all get 24 hours in a day to spend. What really defines us as individuals is how we invest that time. This is a total of 1440 minutes! How are you spending your time? We often put things off, waiting till we get the time, or the perfect time. Unfortunately for some people, that time never comes.

How much would it be worth to find more time in every week?

We live in a world of fast.

We live in a world of fast, don't we? We want everything now, straight away—instant coffee is not quick enough for us any more. How can you get things done without needing any extra time? Look for opportunities to merge activities. If you can pick up 10 minutes here and 10 minutes there, before you know it you've picked up an hour. How much is an hour worth to you in a society that runs at a million miles an hour?

People often ask me how I fit so much into a day, so here are some simple ideas for folding activities into one another. First, stop listening to the radio while you are driving. Put on a CD that adds value to your life. It might be music, a presenter giving you some ideas on how to live your life differently or an audiobook. Why not treat your car as a mobile university?

I listen to my iPod or iPhone whether I'm on a plane, going for a run or on the treadmill at the gym. This is a great way to multitask and create time. I save time by making phone calls from the car or when walking the dog. I also have walking meetings with staff and sometimes even my clients!

Research has shown that we talk to our kids on average about seven minutes a day. Find an opportunity to combine an activity with a conversation. Why not carve out more time with your kids by having them help while you are cooking dinner or a barbecue, so you are making connections with them and strengthening your relationships, or get some exercise together, walk and talk.

At the end of every day, take 10 minutes to create a to-do list for the following day, highlighting the top three things you need to do. When you start work the next morning, you won't waste valuable time working out the priorities for the day.

Authors are often asked where they find the time to write a book. Not surprisingly, books don't write themselves. Writing a book was something I have wanted to do for a long time, so this year I made it a priority and I found the time. If you want something badly enough then you will find the time to make it happen.

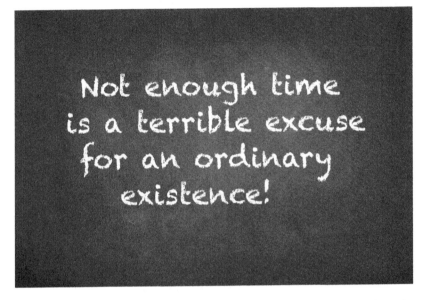

Not enough time
is a terrible excuse
for an ordinary
existence!

Stolen minutes here and there are how you create more time in your day. Stop the excuses and start stealing your time back. A fantastic way to get more time and therefore more done is to put your television in a cardboard box, tape it up and leave it at a friend's house for a few months. You will be surprised at just how much time you waste being entertained by the flat screen.

It is **what** you do, not when you do it, that really **counts**.

Lie 2: too old or too young

It is *never* too late, nor is it ever too early, to start to play a bigger game. Forget age. Clearly it is what you do, not when you do it, that really counts.

We begin by saying to ourselves, 'Oh I'm too young to make a million dollars'; 'I'm too young to train for the Olympics'; 'It's too early to start my own business'; 'I'm not ready to give it a go'; and time slips by and we continually put it off. Before we know it we are starting to say we're too old now; it's too late; somehow the time just disappeared and our dreams never became reality. Age is just a number; it's how you think and feel physically and mentally that matters. Look at Jessica Watson. The youngest person to sail solo round the world in 2010 at just 16 years of age, she proved she was definitely mature enough to take up the challenge.

At the other end of the scale you have Mick Jagger, lead singer of the Rolling Stones, performing at the 2011 Grammy Awards at the age of 67, having an amazing time dancing across the stage and taking the show by storm, just as he did in his twenties.

Look at these examples of individuals, young and old, who have achieved amazing things:

- Mozart wrote his first symphony at age 7.

- At age 14 Nadia Comaneci scored seven perfect 10s in gymnastics at the Montreal Olympics.

- Shane Gould was 16 years old when she won three Olympic gold medals.

- At age 24 Mark Sinclair became the youngest person to have completed a marathon in each continent.

- At age 43 John F. Kennedy became president of the US.

- William Pitt the Younger became prime minister of Britain at age 24, having declined the role the previous year.

- George Foreman became the heavyweight boxing champion of the world at 45.

- Martina Navratilova returned to Wimbledon and represented the US at the 2004 Athens Olympics when she was 47.

- Ray Kroc founded McDonald's at age 53.

- The Rolling Stones became the highest grossing revenue earners for a world tour when they were in their mid sixties.

- In May 2008 Katsusuke Yanagisawa became the oldest person ever to climb Mt Everest. He was 72 years old.

- Ruth Rothfarb started running at the age of 72 because she was 'tired of all the boring talk at funerals' and ran her first marathon at 81.

- Pablo Picasso continued to paint prolifically until his death at age 93.

- Leopold Stokowski was conducting and recording music until his death at age 95. He signed a six-year recording contract at age 94.

- George Burns continued to appear on stage and screen until his death. His last film appearance was at age 98.

- Manoel de Oliveira directed 16 films after he turned 90.

- Composer Elliot Carter has been active through his nineties. His latest work premiered recently at his 100th birthday concert.

- Stage director George Abbott's last Broadway credit was directing a revival of his own play *Broadway* at the age of 100.

- The oldest mayor in the US was Dorothy Geeben, who held office in Ocean Breeze Park, Florida, when she was 100.

Forget age! The best time to do what you want to do is right now.

It is **never** too late or too early to play a bigger **game**.

Lie 3: too busy

If you want something badly enough, you can make it happen. It's very easy to be busy doing nothing. It is very easy to fill your daily schedule with 'stuff' that keeps you away from achieving your goals. Some people make 'busy' an excuse for not doing what they really need to do. For instance, a parent might say, 'I'm too busy to go to the gym. I have to pick up my children from child care.' Could that be an excuse? Let's see:

- ✍ Does the gym you attend have a crèche? Is it possible to pick up your children early from child care and include the gym at the end or the beginning of the day?

- ✍ Do you have to pick your children up every day or is there a family member or friend who could take on that responsibility once or twice a week to free up your time?

- ✍ Why not take your children for a walk or a bike ride in the park after you pick them up from child care? It might not be the gym, but you will be spending quality time with your children and getting some exercise at the same time.

Sometimes being busy is just a convenient excuse. If you truly want to do something, you will manage to fit it in. By staying 'busy' doing nothing in particular, you actually avoid making decisions about things that are way more important in your life. These might include:

- ✍ I'm too busy to clean my room; it will just have to stay the way it is (even though removing clutter is something you constantly talk about).

- ✍ I'm too busy to make those sales calls. (In this case, a fear of rejection may be stopping you from picking up the phone and making the calls, even though if you don't achieve your sales targets your job may be at risk.)

- ✍ I'm too busy to speak to my teenage children about coming home late at night. (If you don't have that conversation and set some boundaries, it's inevitable the poor behaviour will continue.)

You get the picture? Many people pretend they're busy to avoid doing something they don't want to do. Sometimes it's fear that stops them; sometimes it's laziness or procrastination. Whatever the reason, if you want something badly enough, you will always find time to do whatever it takes.

Lie 4: not enough money

People who say they don't have enough money may be guilty of:

- buying things they don't need
- spending money they don't have by using credit
- buying things simply to impress people.

There is always a way to create money. To get you started from zero you will need:

- a budget and a savings plan
- a timeline to work to
- a very clear idea of the reason you want the item(s)
- a true desire to make it happen (see chapter 10)
- persistence
- patience
- willpower.

If you are really unsure of where to start:

- Seek advice from a financial planner or your bank—they can get you started on the road to achieving your financial plans.
- Ask for help.
- Start sooner rather than later. If you can save just $5 a day by, say, giving up coffee or some other small expense and you invest it at just 5 per cent interest, it would be worth $10 588 in five years or $24 102 in 10 years.

Start **sooner** rather than **later**.

Lie 5: not enough knowledge or information

There has never been a better time to seek out information. We are one click away from finding almost limitless information. We can research using Google and other search engines on the internet and find everything we need to know. I recently Googled 'How to learn Spanish' and got 21 000 000 results in 0.25 seconds. That is unbelievable!

We can ask questions and get answers on just about anything. We can track and communicate with people via LinkedIn, Facebook, Twitter and a dozen other social media platforms—the world is our oyster.

You can study pretty much anything at any time, 24 hours a day, seven days a week. With all the online programs now offered by universities and TAFE colleges, you can easily fit your study times around your availability. You can complete online development programs with companies across the globe from your home or office.

You can get apps for your phone that will help you do all sorts of incredible things. Learn a second language, lose weight, get fit, prepare a budget. Instant advice and information in your pocket.

At www.playabiggergame.com.au you can find all the inspiration, motivation and agitation to realise your goals. We offer interviews with successful people, create videos about getting results, maintain a blog about high achievers and send out a newsletter with tips and ideas on how to achieve more, be more, do more and have more—all for free.

There is no excuse for not being able to track down every piece of information you need to achieve your wildest dreams. But you will never play a bigger game if you continue to live by these five lies. Stop using them as a reason why you can't be the best person you can possible be. Get on with your development and growth towards becoming a superstar.

Ryan—rediscovering a passion

Every year I run a series of seminars in each capital city. These forums about playing a bigger game are attended by hundreds of people.

Ryan attended one of these seminars with his partner. I didn't know Ryan and only learned of his story and the impact the seminar had on him when his partner sent me an email inviting me to a CD launch for Ryan's new album. I went along, met his partner, Dianne, and we got chatting about how the album came about.

She told me she had convinced Ryan to come to my seminar because he was the most talented and gifted musician she had met and the love of her life. He had been going gangbusters as a musician in a band with a few mates and was attracting a lot of attention, but just when they looked like breaking through one of the guys got married and dropped out of the band. They spent ages looking for a replacement but when they found one he didn't fit in well, which caused another band member to leave. Then the whole thing unravelled, the band fell apart and Ryan threw in the towel.

Dianne knew he absolutely loved music and she couldn't believe he had just given up. She thought the seminar might help him reawaken his passion for music. Evidently it did, because I was now at the launch of his new CD.

What was the trigger? Ryan came to realise he needed to own his outcomes, rather than let circumstances shape his life. He needed to choose how he responded to circumstances.

You cannot always change circumstances, but you can choose the attitude you have towards them. This allows you to choose your behaviours or actions in response to them. Ryan had let the circumstances (the band falling apart) shape the result (no more music). When he decided to own the results, choose his attitude (I can and I will make this happen) and then create the actions (find a group as passionate about music as he is, who were prepared to make it a priority in their lives), the CD came about pretty quickly. But more importantly, Ryan had rekindled his passion and enthusiasm for what he loved.

Chapter 8 summary

🖒 There are five great lies we tell ourselves that prevent us from developing. These are:

- *Not enough time.* Make time. You have the same amount of time as anyone else; use it wisely. It's easy to find an hour.

- *Too old or too young.* Rubbish! Age is just a number.

- *Too busy.* Get your priorities right. If you want something badly enough, you will find the time.

- *Not enough money.* Create a new financial strategy. There are lots of ways to find money.

- *Not enough knowledge.* Search for it. We live in the information age. You can learn anything. There is no longer any excuse for not being able to track down every piece of information required to achieve your wildest dreams.

MY GAME PLAN:

....

....

....

....

....

....

....

....

....

....

....

....

....

....

....

Chapter 9
Beware the
dream
stealers

Dream stealers are the people who have never done anything, yet they're experts on everything. They want to hold you back and stop you stepping out of the cotton wool because you might prove to be a little better than them: you might achieve a bit more, be a little bit more successful, do something they haven't done. The dream stealers want to pull you back into the cotton wool so you won't move away from them and leave them behind in their average space.

Dream stealers are the people who have never done anything, yet they're **experts** on everything.

You bump into the dream stealers every day. How many people have come into your life and told you, you shouldn't do that; that's not a good idea; don't go there; don't try that; that won't work; you can't do that?

Some American scientists did an experiment in which they put a group of monkeys in a room with a set of stairs and at the top of the stairs was a bunch of bananas. When the monkeys climbed the first stair they were hit with strong jets of icy cold water, from which they shrank back into the corner, cold and shivering. They sat there until they warmed up, then they went for the bananas again, but as soon as they touched the stair the cold water hit them again, and once again they retreated into the corner.

The same scenario was repeated again and again until eventually none of the monkeys would set foot on the stairs. The scientists then removed one of the monkeys from the room and put in a new monkey. He stood there looking at his mates, thinking, 'Don't know what's wrong with you but there are bananas over there', and headed for the bananas, but before he could set foot on the stairs the other monkeys grabbed him and dragged him back. Every time that monkey went near the stairs they grabbed him because they knew what was going to happen, until he too no longer tried for the bananas.

The scientists repeated this exercise until all five monkeys in the room had never experienced the icy water. Even though none of the monkeys had been sprayed with the jets of cold water, not one would try for the bananas.

Now I wonder how many 'monkeys' you have in your life saying, don't go there; don't do that; don't try this, even though they haven't experienced it themselves. They have never bothered to get off their backside and give it a go but they are happy to steal your dreams by giving you all the reasons why you couldn't, wouldn't or shouldn't achieve your dreams.

Not only do we have colleagues, friends and family members in our lives who try to steal our dreams, but we can be our own dream stealers. There are several ways in which we steal our own dreams, sabotaging our own achievements.

Fear

One way we steal our own dreams is through fear: we have this fear of leaving the safety of the cotton wool, fear of stepping out and stepping up. If we try something that no-one else has tried and it doesn't work out, then we'll be labelled a failure. We're afraid we won't be good enough, strong enough or dedicated enough to finish it. We also fear that it might be too challenging, too hard, so we're better off staying safely wrapped up inside that cotton wool, just being average.

Ultimately the only way to overcome fear is either to do the research and investigation needed for what you want to achieve, to build up the necessary knowledge and confidence to make it possible, or to jump in the deep end, give it a go and see what happens. We live in a world that changes so quickly that sometimes you need to learn and adjust on the go—just get started and see what unfolds. Sometimes you don't need to know, you just need to go.

Jump in the **deep end**, give it a go and **see** what happens.

Labels

We also steal our own dreams when we accept labels from other people. People tell us we're something and we accept it's true and live our lives with that label. It starts right from the day we're born—she is really clever; he loves his food.

We get labels at school—he's good at maths; she's a good runner; he can't spell. Then we go to work and we get more labels—he is arrogant; she's not a good leader—and we accept all these labels and they weigh us down as we carry them from job to job, from relationship to relationship. We must be able to shrug off these labels, get rid of them. We need to believe in who we are today, not who someone thinks we have been in the past. What labels are you carrying around that either were never true or are no longer true?

Excuses

Another thing we do when stealing our own dreams is we make excuses. It's easy in this cotton wool society to make excuses. Think of the last time you or someone close to you said they were going to lose weight. 'Starting Monday I'm going to go on a diet and not eat any fatty foods.' After a few successful days, at afternoon tea you're faced with that last chocolate biscuit and you say, 'One biscuit won't hurt!' And the next thing you know you've eaten a whole packet.

Or maybe you decide to give up alcohol and while in a bar at a conference, drinking orange juice or soda water, someone says, 'Come on, have one chardonnay', and the tenth time they say it you give in. 'One won't hurt.' Two hours later you're dancing on the table drinking tequila. And later you say, 'It wasn't working anyway' or 'I wouldn't have made it in the long run'. It's easy to give yourself an excuse to give up, and the more often you do it the easier it becomes.

If you have a history of talking yourself out of being amazing by creating convenient excuses for not getting a result, it's time to toughen up, bite your lip and get on with it, no matter what—no excuses, no complaints, no wishy-washy explanations or cover-ups. Just get the job done. There is one thing worse than lying to others, and that's lying to yourself.

False achievements

The other thing we do is create a false sense of achievement. The cotton wool society encourages us to give people pats on the back when they don't deserve it. We get into the habit of telling our colleagues that they're doing a great job even when we don't really believe that's true. You go to a restaurant and have a bad meal and the waiter asks, 'Was everything okay?' and you say, 'Yeah, fine thanks.' But secretly you're thinking, I'm never coming back. Does this sound familiar?

We've lost the ability to be honest. We tell our kids, 'You're the best dancer I've ever seen!' when we know they're not. We've picked up this false idea that patting people on the back when they don't deserve it is how to encourage them to be awesome. My family will tell you that that's not what happens in our house.

I have four children. I love those kids more than life itself. They are the best thing that ever happened to me. But my children will tell you that in our house you don't get a pat on the back you don't deserve. Don't get me wrong, I encourage them, coach them and help them out in any and every possible way I can, but I have never told them they were fantastic at something when they weren't, because they'd pay for that later in life. If you tell a kid they're fantastic at something ('You're the best singer I've ever heard') and then they audition for the school choir and are rejected, they understandably feel confused and respond accusingly, 'But Daddy, you said I was great.'

So my kids will tell you that if we had a race around the block and I won, then I won. When we played a game it was a real competition. They're paying me back today through video games. Have you ever played video games with kids? I'm getting thrashed and they have no hesitation in pointing it out to me: 'Dad I won, I won. No pats on the back, Dad.' They have grown into wonderful young adults with a true understanding of what it takes to play a bigger game. No false beliefs in what they can do, but a true understanding of what they are capable of and good at doing.

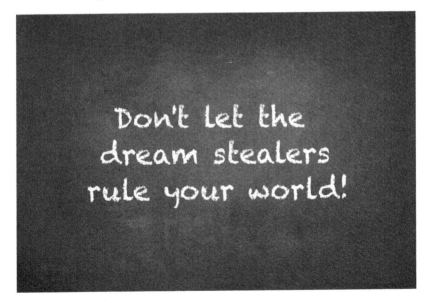

If we let the dream stealers (whether ourselves or the people around us) rule over us, we wouldn't have a lot of the little things we take for granted—simple inventions the dream stealers would have described as stupid, like the paper clip or liquid paper. Some dream stealers even thought computers would be useless. Tom Watson, chairman of IBM in 1958, said, 'I think there is a world market for about five computers'. How wrong was he! Hewlett-Packard tried to steal the dreams of Steve Jobs when they rejected him as an employee. 'We don't need you. You haven't finished college yet', they told him. He went on to found Apple computers.

If we let the dream stealers rule, we wouldn't have a lot of the big things either. India would still be ruled by the British. Nelson Mandela would still be in prison. If we let the dream stealers rule, the Berlin Wall would still divide Germany, John F. Kennedy would never have realised his dream of putting a man on the moon. If we let the dream stealers rule, Martin Luther King Jr's dream of having a black man in the White House would never have happened.

I heard a great story about a young surf lifesaving ironman who said to his good mate one day, 'I'm going to beat The King this year', 'The King' being the current ironman champion. His mate laughed and said, 'Mate you're good, honestly you're good, you're in the top 10, but you're not that good. You'll never beat The King.'

The young ironman turned and walked out of the bar and did not speak to his mate again for three years. Not a word, not a phone call, nothing. Three years later he won the Australian Ironman title, beating the guy he and his mate had referred to as 'The King'.

That afternoon, he walked into the bar and walked up to his old mate and said, 'How you going, mate?'

His mate responded, 'You have a hide! You haven't spoken to me for three years and then you walk in here like you're my best buddy.'

The new champion responded, 'You are my best buddy'.

His mate asked, 'How come you haven't spoken to me for three years?'

The champ replied, 'Because I had a dream; I had a passion; I had a purpose; I had somewhere I was going and you didn't believe in me. So I just couldn't put myself in your space during that time. It doesn't mean I don't think you're the best bloke I know. It just means that for three years while I pursued my dream, I couldn't spend time with somebody who didn't believe in me.'

Don't let the **dream** stealers **rule**.

If you let the dream stealers rule, you'll never get off the path of average and onto the path of awesome to play a bigger game. If you don't get off your backside and start to do something different and get outside the cotton wool society, then you will remain on the loop of the average for the rest of your life.

Rowdy — breaking free of the dream stealers

As a 15 year old, I left my home town with dreams of becoming a professional footballer and a millionaire. I dreamt of coming home a raging success story with all the trappings of wealth and prosperity. Some people laughed and poked fun at me, privately convinced I would be back in no time, with nothing in my pockets and a good dose of humility.

The dream stealers tried to undermine my hopes and dreams. They had never seen anyone achieve what I wanted to achieve, and they didn't think it likely that I would succeed where they hadn't. And to be honest, there were times when I thought they had been right and that I should pull my head in. A voice in my head said, go back to the bush and live an average life. Build a life around just getting by and playing golf on Saturdays.

Not for me, though. I think I was born with an overdose of determination and discipline (my family and friends call it stubbornness), and this is what carried me through to the goals I wanted.

There was no way I was going to let the dream stealers swallow my dreams. In fact, they made me more determined. I wanted to prove them wrong, and I did. When you declare your hopes and dreams to others, you need to be prepared for some people to try to pull them to shreds. Use this as yet another driver for getting what you want.

Chapter 9 summary

- ✍ Dream stealers are the people who have never done anything yet are experts on everything.

- ✍ We can be our own dream stealers.

- ✍ Overcome your fears.

- ✍ Get rid of the labels.

- ✍ Stop making excuses.

- ✍ Encourage real achievement by avoiding false feedback.

- ✍ Don't let the dream stealers rule.

MY GAME PLAN:

....

....

....

....

....

....

....

....

....

....

....

....

....

....

....

Chapter 10
Make it
happen

In the next few pages we are going to walk through the process of making your goals a reality. It's a simple process that you can repeat time and time again to get what you really want out of life. The play a bigger game matrix is far more than just a goal-setting exercise; it's a comprehensive model that will help you make the impossible possible. It takes all the elements of playing a bigger game and combines them into one comprehensive document that will have you achieving real results in no time.

The play a **bigger** game matrix is a **blueprint** for your **future**.

The desire for more is the most powerful desire in our culture (*Fast Company*, March 2003). For the past decade I have run motivational seminars for thousands of people around the globe. The people who attend these seminars are people who have the drive to achieve more, be more, do more and have more. As part of this seminar we survey participants on what are the biggest barriers to their success. The main barrier, according to an overwhelming 93 per cent of respondents, is 'me'. It seems the person you see in the mirror each morning is the biggest barrier to your getting what you want out of life. Most people just can't get up the courage, find the time or develop the tools to break through the barriers to changing their lives for the better. Most people struggle to get out of their own way. The great news is that if you are the problem, you are also the solution. This book will help you take control and make the things you really want in life happen.

I am not a fan of goal setting—writing down your hopes and dreams and putting them on a shelf or in a drawer, then, years down the track, discovering the list and wondering why you never did anything about it.

I *am* a fan of goal kicking—writing down your goals and then creating a set of actions to make them come true. Most people fail at goal setting because they treat it more as a wish list, with no follow-through or accountability. The number one reason people fail to achieve more, be more, do more and have more is not that they do not have goals but that they do not take action to achieve them.

It's a comprehensive **model** that will **help** you make the impossible possible.

In order to kick our goals we need to create a blueprint to ensure we not only keep them in focus but become aware of the key drivers in making our goals real.

In this chapter we are going to use a razor-sharp focus to allow us to create a clear vision of the opportunities and possibilities that lie ahead for you!

The play a bigger game matrix will help you:

- understand what it is you should focus on
- know why it is important to you
- create an action plan for making it a reality.

Before we start on the matrix, which will focus on your short-term future, let's give some thought to your long-term future. You need to have a vision of where you want to be in the long run so you can create short-term goals to get you there.

Where will you be in five years?

Let's start this exercise by thinking deeply about where you will be, and what you want to have achieved, five years from today.

5 YEARS = 260 WEEKS = 1820 DAYS = 2 622 240 MINUTES

What will you do with it? Some people have difficulty imagining what life might be like in five years' time. I want you to think about what you would really like:

- ✍ Where do you live?

- ✍ What sort of job do you have?

- ✍ How is your health?

- ✍ How are your relationships with your family, friends and colleagues?

- ✍ How stable are your finances?

- ✍ What makes you happy?

It's amazing what can be achieved in just five years if you choose to begin now.

Consider **what** you want, *really* want in **life**.

Let me give you some idea of the possibilities...

- ✍ In less than five years Shakespeare wrote *Hamlet*, *Othello*, *King Lear*, *Macbeth* and five other immortal plays.

- ✍ In just under five years, Michelangelo painted the breathtaking ceiling of the Sistine Chapel.

- ✍ Most Olympic medallists rise from obscurity to awesome in less than five years. Emily Seebohm, Cate Campbell (swimming) and Melissa Wu (diving) were all only 16 years of age when they were members of the Australian 2008 Olympic team.

👍 Amazon.com founder Jeff Bezos went from living in a 500 square foot apartment at the age of 30 to having a net worth of $10 billion just five years later.

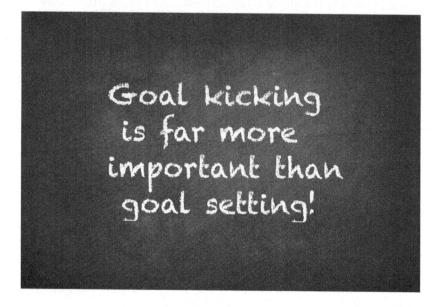

Goal kicking is far more important than goal setting!

Do goals really matter?

Goals, particularly when they are written down, possess an explosive power to bring dreams to life. Nowhere has this been better illustrated than in a recent study by Dr Gail Matthews at Dominican University. This research involved participants from the US, Belgium, the UK, India, Australia and Japan, and included entrepreneurs, educators, healthcare professionals, artists, lawyers, bankers, marketers, human services providers, managers and directors of non-profit organisations. In this study participants with written goals were found to be 50 per cent more likely to achieve their goals than those with unwritten goals.

Actor Jim Carrey took written goals to another level, as he revealed on *The Oprah Winfrey Show*. Carrey had once had a goal of earning a million dollars for a movie role. At the time he set this goal he was making barely $20 000 a year. So he wrote himself a million-dollar cheque and he kept it in his wallet. Every single day he would see the cheque and visualise 'owning' the money. Two years later he signed up for the movie *Dumb and Dumber* and was paid a million dollars for the role. Jim Carrey showed the audience the tattered old cheque that he had carried with him for those two years.

It has been proved that writing down your goals gives you a greater chance of success, but it's not enough simply to have written goals. Obviously you need to know *where* you want to go, but you also need a good, clear plan on *how* you are going to get there. That's why goal kicking is far more effective than goal setting—because it gives you the plan, not just the destination.

Perhaps the thought of the five years ahead overwhelms you. Let's change our focus from five years to a 90-day time frame. Why set 90-day goals? I have spent years looking for the optimum time frame for the realisation of something you truly want to achieve. I've tried every variation, from 30 days to 12 months. Thirty days is just too short to really get momentum going to achieve results. But once we get beyond 90 days the goals seem to get lost in everyday life; we lose focus and our goals don't get the attention they need.

The great thing about 90 days is that once you get used to executing a goal in 90 days and realise how easy it is, you can actually repeat the process. In 12 months you have four 90-day periods to execute your top four goals. How awesome would it be to achieve four significant chosen objectives each year? That would see you playing a bigger game.

To play a bigger game, we want you to achieve one goal every 90 days over the next 12 months, but first we have to find out what it is you really want to achieve and help you identify the most important goal for you to focus on over the next 90 days. Then we will show you how to achieve four goals over the year.

Figure 10.1 presents the play a bigger game matrix. This is the key to helping you decide on your future for the next 90 days. In figure 10.2 (p. 106) we have reproduced part of the matrix at a size that gives you plenty of space to write in. Let's start with these five squares in figure 10.2. In five minutes, write down five things you would like to achieve in the next 90 days, using no more than 10 words for each. The idea is to make this exercise as short, sharp and concise as possible.

If you are struggling to come up with five goals, you might consider the 'four pillars' of life: health, relationships, career and finances. These four pillars are fundamental to playing a bigger game. Most people want more of something in one or more of these key areas.

Don't spend too much time deciding. Generally, the things that pop into your head as soon as you ask the question are the things you really want in your life. If you do the exercise quickly, there won't be time for all the *shoulds* to come up. Often the *shoulds* are things other people want you to do, not what you yourself truly want. Any statement with a *should* in it or a *should* as the reason behind it actually belongs to someone else.

🖒 My boss has decided I should get a degree.

🖒 My parents believe I should buy a house.

🖒 My partner thinks I should cut back my work hours.

But this is about *you*, not them, and the reality is if you don't really want what they want, you won't put in the effort or focus as well as if you own the outcome. So drop the *shoulds*, just stick with the five things *you* want in your life in the next 90 days.

Figure 10.1: the play a bigger game matrix

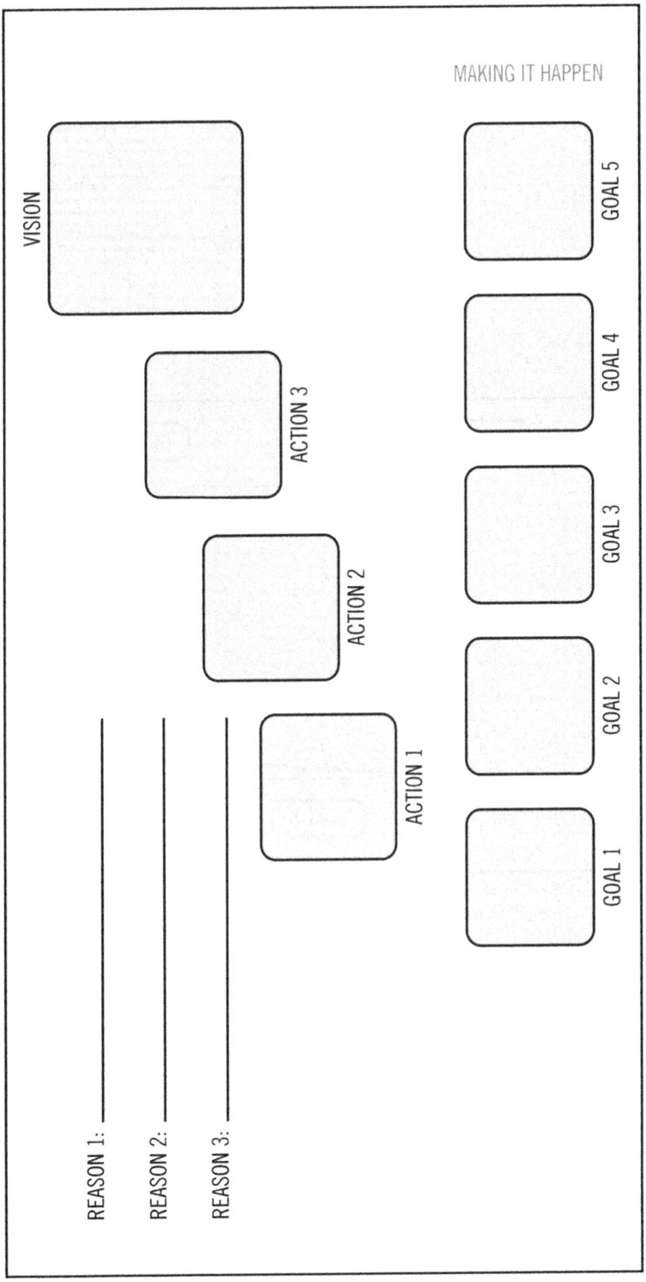

MAKING IT HAPPEN

VISION

ACTION 3

ACTION 2

ACTION 1

GOAL 5

GOAL 4

GOAL 3

GOAL 2

GOAL 1

REASON 1: _____

REASON 2: _____

REASON 3: _____

Figure 10.2: the play a bigger game matrix goals section — your 90-day goals

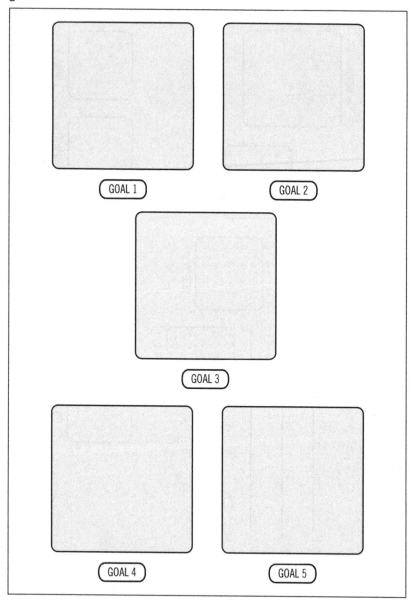

Let's take the example of Paul, an under-40 dad with two school-age children under six. His partner works part-time; he is paying off a mortgage and planning a family holiday. Paul has neglected his fitness plans in the past few years and is paying the price with his health now. He is unhappy with his job because he thinks he is being taken for granted by the company he works for.

Paul has written five 90-day goals:

1 *Spend more time with my children.*

2 *Improve my relationship with my partner.*

3 *Get fit and lose 10 Kg.*

4 *Find a better job.*

5 *Take a family holiday.*

Paul knows there are a stack of things he would like in his life, but these are the five things he really wants to achieve now.

Now let's look at Sandy, a single, under-30 middle manager based in San Francisco. She works long hours, feels like she's living on a treadmill—work, sleep, work, sleep. She hasn't been out for ages, her social life is nonexistent and she badly needs a holiday. Her boss is constantly driving her to achieve more and spend more hours at her desk. She likes her job, just not her boss's expectations. But the more work she does, the more work she is given.

Sandy has written five goals for the next 90 days:

1 *Reduce the hours I am working.*

2 *Save $10 000 for a new car.*

3 *Start dating again.*

4 *Take a mini holiday.*

5 *Get fitter and lose 5 Kg.*

It was an effort for Sandy to come up with these five goals. She hasn't thought much further than a few days ahead for ages, as she invests most of her energy in keeping on top of her job. Interestingly, despite her work pressures, she did not include changing her job.

We will come back to Paul's and Sandy's goals in the next chapter as we work our way through the playing a bigger game matrix. Knowing what you really want is just the first step.

Chris — knowing what he wants

Know what you want. You can't get to your destination if you don't know where you want to go. I recently worked with an executive manager of a very large corporation. Chris was, for all intents and purposes, a fairly successful guy. He was well paid, had the respect of his colleagues and employees, and was regarded as third in charge. He had been responsible for the introduction and implementation of some great initiatives in the organisation. Chris had been with the company for over 20 years and was very happy in his role.

The reason I was working with Chris was because his boss had decided he had become comfortable and a little complacent. I spent some time asking Chris a series of questions about his career. His feedback was pretty much as expected — comfortable and confident. Chris knew what was on the horizon next week, next month and even next year, and was confident he could achieve the required results.

The breakthrough came when I asked him where he would be in five years' time. He replied, 'I hope to be in the same position, carrying out the same role.' I asked him how he would feel if the opportunity for promotion came up but he was overlooked for the role. He didn't think that would happen. When I pressed him his response was quite clear: 'There's no way I could work here if someone got that job over me.' The next question was the key:

'If you want the job that badly, are you doing *everything* you can possibly do right now to make it happen?' It was like he'd been slapped across the face. He thought for a moment and then he said, 'You know what, I've been cruising along, doing fine, taking it easy, waiting for the company to give me that job, and I've just realised (1) how badly I want it and (2) that doing what I'm doing won't make it happen. In five years I *will* be second in charge here and I need to stay focused on that.'

Now that Chris knows what he really wants, he is going after it and his boss has noticed the change.

Chapter 10 summary

- ⌂ The desire for more is the most powerful desire in our culture.

- ⌂ Choose goal kicking rather than simply goal setting.

- ⌂ What will be different for you in five years' time?

- ⌂ Writing down your goals matters.

- ⌂ You can achieve something significant in 90 days.

- ⌂ The play a bigger game matrix is a blueprint for your future.

MY GAME PLAN:

Chapter 11
Get your
priorities
right

The next step in playing a bigger game is to decide which goal is the priority for you right now. To get really clear on which of your five 90-day goals is the most important for you, and therefore the one to execute first, we will use a process called *false ranking*. Ideally this exercise should be completed in less than five minutes, because when forced to choose quickly we tend to choose what is important to us now. Asking certain questions about your five goals can help you to resolve which is most important to you.

The false ranking process

False ranking is the process of comparing each of your chosen goals with all the others. The aim is to help you identify your number one, priority goal through a process of elimination. You might be surprised which one of your goals ends up at the top of the list when you have completed this exercise. Let's walk through the process as we ask Paul to compare the five goals he chose.

1 Spend more time with my children.

- 👍 'Paul, is spending time with your children more important than rekindling your relationship with your partner?' Paul chooses improving his relationship with his partner, so let's put a tick beside goal 2 on his list.

- 👍 'Is spending more time with your children more important than getting fit and losing 10 kilos?' Again both are important, but spending time with his children definitely wins out as his priority. Tick beside goal 1.

- 👍 'Okay, next, is spending time with your children more important than finding a better job?' Definitely the children come first. Tick goal 1 again.

- 👍 'Finally, is spending time with your children more important than taking the family on holiday?' The family holiday would probably improve his relationship with his partner and allow him to spend more time with his kids, so he chooses the family holiday. Tick goal 5.

So now let's repeat this exercise with the next item on his list.

2 Improve my relationship with my partner.

- 👍 'Is improving your relationship more important than getting fit?' His relationship is more important, so tick goal 2.

- 👍 'Is improving your relationship more important than getting a better job?' Again, his relationship is more important, so tick goal 2.

- 👍 'Is improving your relationship more important than taking a family holiday?' The holiday is more important, so tick goal 5.

Now we do the same with the next item on the list (note this process gets faster as we work down the list).

> **Progress is not about doing the easy things. Its about doing the right NEXT thing, for you!**

3 Get fit and lose 10 Kg.

👍 'Is getting fit more important than getting a better job?' Getting fit is more important, so tick goal 3.

👍 'Is getting fit more important than taking a family holiday?' The holiday is more important, so tick goal 5.

Finally:

👍 'Is getting a better job more important than going on a family holiday?' Paul chooses the holiday, so puts another tick next to goal 5.

That's it. We have now compared the importance of each of the five goals against the others. This is how Paul's list now looks:

1 Spend more time with my children. ✓✓

2 Improve my relationship with my partner. ✓✓✓

3 Get fit and lose 10 Kg. ✓

4 Find a better job.
5 Take a family holiday. ✓✓✓✓

As you can see, Paul's number one priority is to arrange a family holiday for his kids and partner.

After comparing each individual goal against each other goal, the most important one ends up with the most ticks. *Let's highlight that goal with a highlighter pen or circle it* so we can readily identify Paul's number one goal for the next 90 days.

Let's now apply the false ranking exercise to Sandy's goals. Using the same process, we will ask Sandy the same false ranking questions.

1 Reduce the hours I am working.

👍 'Which is more important, reducing the hours you are working or saving for a new car?' If Sandy doesn't stop working such long hours she will never have time to drive a new car, so she puts a tick next to goal 1 on her list.

👍 'Is it more important to reduce the hours you are working or to start to date again?' Although dating would be great, she has to have the *time* to date, so again she ticks goal 1.

👍 'Now, is working fewer hours more important to you than taking a mini holiday?' Sandy believes that working fewer hours would be like having a mini holiday, so again she ticks goal 1.

👍 'Finally, is working fewer hours more important than getting fit and losing 5 kilos?' Currently her long work hours leave no time for the gym, so working fewer hours remains a priority. Tick goal 1 again.

Now let's move on to compare Sandy's second goal with the rest of her list:

👍 'Is saving for a new car more important than starting dating again?' Sandy chooses dating, so tick goal 3.

🖒 'Is saving for a new car more important than having a mini holiday?' The holiday is more important, so tick goal 4.

🖒 'Is saving for a new car more important than getting fit?' Losing weight is more important right now, so tick goal 5.

Let's finish off by comparing the last few:

🖒 'Is starting to date again more important than having a mini holiday?' Dating is more important, so tick goal 3.

🖒 'Is starting to date again more important than getting fit and losing 5 kilos?' Losing weight is more important, so tick goal 5.

Finally:

🖒 'Is having a mini holiday more important than getting fit and losing 5 kilos?' Getting fit is more important, so Sandy ticks goal 5.

Here are Sandy's full results:

1 Reduce the hours I am working. ✓✓✓✓

2 Save $10 000 for a new car. ✓✓

3 Start dating again. ✓✓

4 Take a mini holiday. ✓

5 Get fitter and lose 5 Kg. ✓✓✓

Clearly, Sandy's priority for the next 90 days is to reduce the number of hours she is working.

Now it's your turn. Just as we did with Paul and Sandy, ask yourself the question, 'Is my current goal 1 more important than my goal 2?' Remember, this false ranking exercise should take you less than five minutes. Again, don't stress with the process. Trust that you will make the right decision and confidently select the goal that is your number one priority.

Write your five goals below, then use the false ranking method to find your highest priority goal.

1 ....
....

2 ....
....

3 ....
....

4 ....
....

5 ....
....

Once you have eliminated the other four goals, highlight your number one goal with a highlighter pen or by circling it. If you have two goals with an equal number of ticks, choose which one of these you believe is most important. That will be your highest priority.

Congratulations! Part of playing a bigger game is knowing exactly where you want to go and being clear on why you want to go there.

Part of playing a **bigger** game is knowing exactly where **you** want to go.

Our research shows that if you strive to achieve all five goals in the next 90 days, you will likely find it a struggle and become overwhelmed. In trying to achieve all five you may actually achieve none. If we focus on just one goal in the next 90 days, we increase our chances tenfold of achieving that goal.

In the next chapter we will show how you can make your number one priority goal happen within the 90 days.

Debbie — defining her priorities

Have you ever been overwhelmed by the list of things you have to do? I once worked with a team on productivity and execution and met a manager named Debbie. My first impression of Debbie was that she looked worn out and seemed at her wit's end. When we talked about getting things done she told me her problem wasn't an inability to get things done. Her problem was that as soon as she got things done people gave her *more* things to do. It seemed the old saying 'If you want something done, give it to a busy person' had been taken to heart by her colleagues and they had no problem with passing on more and more work to Debbie.

Now Debbie liked to be busy. What stressed her out was trying to work out what the next thing to do was. When your to-do sheet is as long as your arm it's hard to stay focused and easy to feel overwhelmed.

So we did the simple exercise you've just read about in this chapter. We got her list down to the five most important tasks for the week on a Monday morning. We then false ranked them to put them in a priority order. Then Debbie went about executing these tasks one by one with complete focus. She told her colleagues that she had her priorities, and that if they had something to add to the list it would have to go on the next priority list.

The result: Debbie got heaps more done, yet she was less stressed and *enjoyed* getting things done. In fact, she now often completes all five priorities in a day and starts a new list each morning.

Chapter 11 summary

👍 False ranking is a great way of identifying priorities.

👍 Focus on achieving one goal in 90 days.

👍 Playing a bigger game is knowing exactly what you want to achieve.

👍 You are more likely to succeed when you focus on just one goal at a time.

MY GAME PLAN:

....

....

....

....

....

....

....
....
....
....
....
....
....
....
....
....
....
....
....
....
....
....

Chapter 12
Make it real—paint the picture

The next step in achieving your goal is to describe the result or outcome as if it was already true and happening today. We have duplicated the large box from the play a bigger game matrix on the next page. Now imagine you have achieved your number one priority goal. In the box in figure 12.1 (p. 126) write down what it will look like, what it will feel like and what impact the change will have on your life. Can you see yourself experiencing that goal? Where are you and what are you doing? Close your eyes if you need to. Try to imagine exactly what the outcome will be and what it might bring to you.

In Paul's case, he is imagining taking a family holiday in Australia. This is what Paul wrote:

> We are at the beach and enjoying the sunshine. We are staying in a two-bedroom beachfront apartment on the tenth floor. The children love the apartment and have taken over the second bedroom. Each morning we

take a walk around the beachfront past Greenmount Beach, Rainbow Bay and a little beach called Froggies, where a big, frog-shaped rock has been painted green. The children love Froggies, playing in the sand and paddling in the ocean. Jane and I walk hand in hand along the beach as the children collect shells, and later we build a sandcastle on the edge of the surf, before the tide comes in and washes it away. There's heaps of laughter and lots of smiles.

We all go out for Mexican for dinner. It's great to sit down as a family and talk about the day. The kids are so excited and having a great time. Jane looks fantastic and is the most relaxed I have seen her for ages. I am as content as I can possibly be.

We head home and the kids fall asleep early after all the activity, Jane and I get to have a glass of wine on the balcony and some lovely, quiet time alone.

I know this is a holiday the family will never forget. I have taken many digital photos and this morning I asked a stranger to take a family shot at the beach. This fantastic *photo will take pride of place on my desk at work as a reminder of the great time we had as a family.*

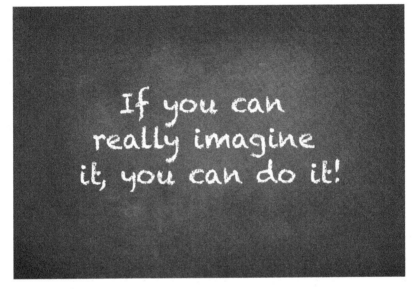

The clearer you are in describing what it will be like when you achieve your priority goal, the better. Paul's description is very vivid — you can almost feel yourself at the beach with the family on holiday.

The **more** detail in the description, the more likely it will become **real**.

Take the time to fill in the box in figure 12.1, overleaf, using as many descriptive words as you can. The clearer your vision of your goal, the better chance you have of achieving it. If you can bring it to life in your description, you will find it much easier to make it real.

By the end of the exercise the entire box will be filled with images, emotions and feelings as you transport yourself to the time when your goal is realised.

Figure 12.1: your vision of your priority goal

Robert — the power of a great imagination

What your mind can conceive you can achieve. I have always been a believer in the power of a great imagination. Our brain is such an amazingly powerful tool. Most of us under-utilise our brains. In fact, I think some people fail to use them at all! I was discussing this topic with one of my clients recently.

Robert was intrigued when I told him that every single success I have ever had I could picture in my mind long before it became a reality. Over the years I have been able to picture in my mind playing professional sport, running my own company, speaking in front of thousands of people, running a marathon, even having this book published.

So Robert decided to put it to the test. He and his wife were looking to buy a new house and hadn't been able to settle on what they really wanted, so they sat down and spent some time writing down in detail what they really wanted. They added more and more detail — things like a pool with an infinity edge and with a view, an en suite with dual basins and separate walk-in robes, a rumpus room with a pool table, a big-screen television and surround sound, and the list went on. Then Robert and I got together and he described the house to me, not from paper but from the picture he had in his head.

Twelve months later Robert and his wife bought a new house and everything they wanted was either in it or could be added to it. To me it appears exactly as Robert described it. The power you have to create reality from pictures you have in your mind is simply amazing. There is one important caveat to this though. Your mind can as easily create bad images as good ones, so try to empty out the bad ones before they take hold and become a reality.

Chapter 12 summary

👍 Our subconscious is great at making pictures in our mind seem real.

👍 Create a picture of the future as if it exists today.

👍 The more detail in the description, the more likely it will become real.

MY GAME PLAN:

....

....

....

....

....

....

....

Make it real—paint the picture

129

....

....

....

....

....

....

....

....

....

....

....

....

....

....

....

Chapter 13
Real reasons
for success

When the why is big enough, the how looks after itself.

Your next step towards realising your goal within 90 days is to list three reasons why this goal is important to you. These are exactly the reasons why you simply *must* make the goal a reality.

What connects this goal to you? In these exercises we are setting up the mental processes to accomplish your goal. We are on our way to playing a bigger game and making certain we achieve the goal within 90 days.

Let's take a look at the reasons Sandy gave for why her goal is important to her. Remember, her priority goal was to reduce the number of hours she works. The reasons this is important to her are, in her words:

'I don't have a life anymore. I chased the corporate dream of "work hard, get promoted quickly" and am still waiting for the payoff.' Her number one reason for this goal is: *she wants a life again!*

'I am disconnected from my old friends and feel that my life is slipping by.' *She wants to reconnect with her friends and family.*

'I have become jaded and unproductive at work because of the long hours. I know I need time off to recharge the batteries. Working fewer hours will help me achieve that.' *She needs a real break.*

What are the reasons why you simply **must** make the goal a **reality**?

Sandy is now very clear on why her goal is important to her. Gaining this knowledge is a critical step to making sure you achieve your priority goal and begin working towards playing a bigger game. When obstacles confront you, it is important that you have a very strong reason—the *why*—for achieving your goal. The *why* is what will keep you going way past day five, day 55 and right through to day 90, when your goal becomes a reality.

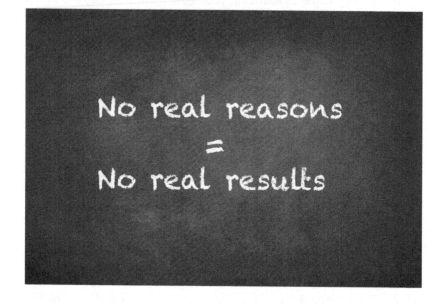

No real reasons
=
No real results

Now it's your turn to focus on your number one goal. What are the three main reasons you *must* achieve your goal? Write your three reasons below—be as clear as possible.

REASON 1: ....

....

....

....

....

REASON 2: ....

....

....

....

....

REASON 3: ....

....

....

....

....

Well done! This goal is really taking shape for you. You are on your way to playing a bigger game!

Wendy — following her own dream

Are you following your dreams or the dreams of someone else? Does the *why* that sits behind what you want to achieve really belong to you, or are you working to make someone else happy?

At one of my seminars we had talked about *why* and the fact that when the why is strong enough the goal almost takes on a life of its own. Afterwards a young woman, Wendy, came up to me and told me her story.

Wendy was studying to be a doctor, but she hated the study; she just didn't have the energy or enthusiasm for it. So I asked her the obvious question: 'Why do it, if you hate it so much?' Wendy's answer was quite simple. Her father and mother were both doctors. Her father's father had been a doctor. Her older brother was a successful surgeon, and the family expectation was that Wendy too would become a doctor or practise medicine in some way.

No-one had even asked Wendy what she wanted. It was just accepted that she would enter the medical profession.

Wendy and I had quite a long chat. It was obvious she had absolutely no passion for medicine but was following that path solely because of pressure from her family. But she wasn't getting good results, which caused further angst as her family offered her all kinds of advice on how she could get better grades. Wendy really wanted to be a journalist. The why behind her current path belonged to her family, not to her.

I suggested she had to sit down with her family, tell them what she really wanted to do and why, show them some of her work (she had some articles published in magazines under a false name).

I never heard from Wendy again but one day I happened on an article published in a large metropolitan newspaper that bore her name. It seemed she had finally followed her passion.

Chapter 13 summary

- When the *why* is big enough the *how* looks after itself.

- Emotion connects your goals to reality.

- The *why* is the reason you *must* achieve your goals.

MY GAME PLAN:

....

....

....

....

....

....

....

Chapter 14

No **action,**
no results

The final step in completing our play a bigger game matrix is to execute the action steps, as represented by the three boxes across the middle of the matrix (figure 10.1 on p. 105). In figure 14.1, overleaf, we have expanded these three boxes to allow sufficient room for you to write your responses. These are the most important action steps we can take to start playing a bigger game.

Let's work on the actions you need to implement. Think of the three critical actions you are going to need to take in order to make your goal a reality. Enter the first action in the lowest box on the left, the next action in the middle box and the final action in the top box.

Action is the key to getting results and creating amazing outcomes. We have all heard how actions speak louder than words. It's true. I don't want to hear what you might do—all that hot air about stuff that will never happen. I want to hear what you are doing, what action you are taking to get ahead, to become better, to play a bigger game. Actions are proof that you are in the game; that you're making an effort; that you're determined to make things happen. You cannot talk your way to better results; you have to do the work.

Now, simply writing out these actions will not make them a reality; we need to consider some other elements to ensure we follow through.

Figure 14.1: three critical action steps

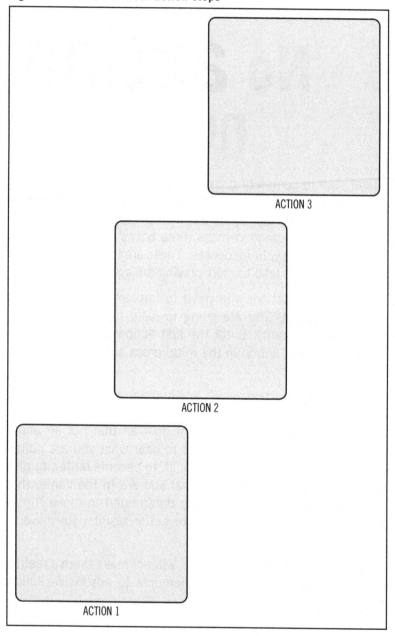

There are three additional elements to every action.

Element 1: the time frame

The first is the time frame. When is the deadline for completing the action, or how often will the action take place? For example, if our goal were to get fit, then how many times would we aim to go to the gym or exercise each week, and what time of day would those workouts take place? Is it the same time slot every day or is it necessary to be flexible to allow for your other commitments?

Having a time frame is your insurance policy against procrastination. There is nothing like a deadline to get you going—a line in the sand that you are committed to. If you share this time frame or deadline with others, they will keep you accountable. They will push your buttons about your commitment and get you worked up about the deadline, and if you're like me you will never miss a commitment you have shared with someone else. That keeps me on top of my game.

Element 2: support

The second element is the support we have or need. What support is available to help you achieve your goal? Support comes in many different forms. The more forms of support you have, the better your chances of making that action a reality.

Firstly, consider *who* can give you support. The last thing you need is someone who will undermine your progress. Is there a family member, close friend, workmate or neighbour who will support and encourage you? Including your supporter(s) in your goal-setting strategy is a great way of ensuring it will happen, particularly if it's someone who will keep you honest and push you a little along the way. When choosing an accountability buddy, steer clear of those people who give in too easily or, even worse, encourage you to give in.

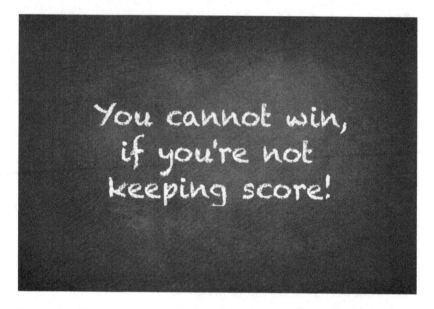

You may also seek out people you can learn from. Mentors and coaches are a fantastic source of support, as they know the strategies that work and the pitfalls that come with them. For example, if your goal is to write a book, one of your action steps might be to seek out the advice of experienced authors. If your action is to start a fitness program, you might start by consulting a personal trainer.

Another support mechanism is information and knowledge. Today we are one click away from a worldwide web of information. You can Google amazing information to help you tailor your actions to exactly what will work best for you. You can read books, magazines, blogs, ezines and ebooks, visit websites, watch videos, and buy DVDs and CDs that will teach you all sorts of things. There is a virtually limitless source of information available to us, so 'I don't know how' is no longer a valid excuse for inaction.

'I don't know **how**' is no longer a valid **excuse** for inaction.

Invest in education and personal development. Get some lessons if necessary. Support might mean attending a workshop or conference with people who can teach you the skills you need. Alternatively, you could go to college or university or study online.

Find out **where** the lesson lies, make the change and get on with playing the **bigger** game.

Element 3: be aware of the obstacles

The third element in ensuring your action step actually happens is making yourself aware of the obstacles you may encounter along the way. What are some of the obstacles that are likely to create barriers to carrying through your action? What are some of the things that got in the way of your achieving it in the past?

For example, you engage a personal trainer three to four times a week, but within a month you find you can't afford that frequency, so you stop the sessions altogether and give up on your fitness program.

An alternative might be to discuss 90-day options with the trainer, who is probably looking for long-term clients. Explain that you want to start three to four times a week for, say, two weeks, then drop back to twice a week for one-on-one sessions, while you continue the additional sessions by yourself, modelling the trainer's program. If you have a plan to overcome the obstacles, they will not sabotage your success.

Or maybe you need to consider what effect a change in the weather or in temperature at the time of the day you start exercising may have on your motivation. For example, will daylight saving influence the time of day you exercise? Is it okay for you to exercise in the dark when the clocks are turned back, or will a cold snap keep you in bed when you should be up and at 'em?

Anticipating potential obstacles before they arise increases your chances of completing the actions. You will be better prepared with a backup plan or strategy for overcoming them.

No **strategy** to overcome obstacles = no **results**.

Write down your three most important action steps in the answer fields provided. There is space for you to specify the steps then address the three elements—time, support and obstacles—relating to each of those steps.

This is a really important part of the play a bigger game matrix, so take the time to clarify your thoughts and plans for this exercise.

Can you see now why setting goals may not have been successful for you in the past? Most people never write down their goals, which means they rarely become real. Those who do usually just write them down and imagine this will somehow magically make them happen. But you have now covered all the bases, which gives you every chance of success. If you take the time to complete the goal-setting matrix, I guarantee you will start to play a bigger game sooner than you think.

ACTION 1: ....

....

....

....

....

....

Time frame: ....

....

Support: ....

....

....

Obstacles: ....

....

....

....

ACTION 2: ....

....

....

....

....

....

....

Time frame: ....

....

....

Support: ....

....

....

Obstacles: ....

....

....

ACTION 3: ....

....

....

....

....

....

....

Time frame: ....

....

....

Support: ....

....

....

Obstacles: ....

....

....

Merv — turning a dream into reality

We have all heard it said that actions speak louder than words. This is so true. It's not what you talk about but what you do that's important.

In my line of work I get to hear some tremendous stories about what people are *going to do*. They are full of enthusiasm and excitement and you get caught up in that initial moment of bountiful hope for what is possible. And to be honest, I think people need that at the beginning to get a kick-start. But when you hear it year after year you start to see through the blind optimism and doubt the person's sincerity.

Every year I go on holiday with some great friends and we have an absolute ball. One of these friends is Merv. Every year we get caught up in the whirlwind of his hopes and dreams — in particular, his desire to go to Tanzania and climb Mt Kilimanjaro. Every year for the past 10 years we have heard the same story delivered with energy and excitement and great earnestness: 'This year I am going to climb Kilimanjaro!' And always there's the same result: too busy, too tired, no time, no money.

Well, this year I got sick of it. Normally I try not to bring my play a bigger game message into the space of my close friendships, but I just couldn't stand it any more. I told Merv that either he did it this year or he should never *ever* mention it again. He looked me in the eye and said, 'You bet, I am definitely doing it.' Of course I didn't believe him, so I asked him what were the three keys actions he had to take to make it a reality. His reply: book a guide, book a flight, prepare. Let's not make this all talk, I said. Let's take action *now*. So, with a little coaxing and some nudges, by the end of the day he had booked a guide, booked and paid for his flights and arranged a training program with a personal trainer with an altitude chamber in his gym.

The great news is that Merv actually stayed committed, followed through and this year realised his dream of standing on top of Kilimanjaro. When we got together afterwards he confided in me that if I had not forced him to take action, his dream would probably only ever have been words.

It's great to come up with a vision, but dreams without action will always remain dreams.

Chapter 14 summary

- Actions speak louder than words.
- Actions make goals real.
- Set at least three critical actions for every goal.
- Each action needs a time frame.
- Be aware of the support available to execute your actions.
- Create strategies for overcoming obstacles.

MY GAME PLAN:

....

....

....

....

....

....

....

....

....

....

....

....

....

....

....

Chapter 15
Work smarter, not harder

If you have reached this stage of the book there is a great chance that you are actually prepared to do whatever it takes to get what you want out of life. According to publishing services firm Jenkins Group, only 57 per cent of books are read to completion. If you have come this far, you obviously believe in yourself. You have a vision for what is possible and a desire to execute the actions required to get what you want. You are committed.

Once you are truly committed to making changes to get the results you want there are some powerful things you can do to leverage that commitment, to step things up a level and gain some extra momentum. These are the tools I used to fast-track my success.

Peer group

Surround yourself with people who are playing a bigger game. Find people who want the same things out of life you do. It's easy to get caught up with a group of people going nowhere, because like-minded people are attracted to one another and tend to hang out together.

Often people in poor relationships get together and complain about their partners. People who are overweight hang out in fast-food outlets. Fitness fanatics get together with other fitness fanatics. Rich people hang out with rich people. We tend to mix with people who support and reinforce our behaviours.

So take a good look at the people you spend most of your time with and consider whether they are pulling you up or dragging you down. If you are genuinely interested in stepping up, successful people will give you a hand. Recently I was chatting with a mate of mine, Stuart, who five years ago had started a healthy food franchise that has made him a multimillionaire. So I asked him what the best strategy he had used to get there was. He said he had created a list of the top 100 franchise CEOs and contacted them to see if they would have coffee with him. More than 50 per cent said yes. Why? Because Stuart conveyed his passion, enthusiasm and desire to succeed. He chose to mix with individuals who had played or were playing the bigger game that he wanted to play.

Surround yourself with people who are playing a bigger game.

When you genuinely want to make a change for the better, and you communicate that, people are quite generous.

Search for the heroes

Another great strategy I used was to look for the heroes in my life—people who embodied what I wanted to become. People who had the values I admired, who had the sort of success I wanted to pursue. People who had been there and done that.

I made a list of those people and then studied what they did and how they did it. I looked at how they behaved when things got tough. I looked at the key things that helped them achieve their goals. If they had published I bought their books; if they had a website I explored it; if they had videos I watched them; if they had an online course I bought it.

I listened to interviews; I read blogs; I did everything I could to get to understand the things they did to achieve more, be more, do more and have more. It's amazing the simple short cuts you can find by studying someone who has already made the journey you are about to embark on. It's easy to study heroes, famous people such as Nelson Mandela, Oprah Winfrey, Bill Gates, Richard Branson, Kelly Slater, Venus and Serena Williams, Mark Zuckerberg, Bono, Lady Gaga or whoever is an expert or especially successful in your own field.

It's amazing the **simple** shortcuts you can find by studying someone who has already made the **journey**.

I also found it useful to spend time with the successful people who are not so famous. I remember that as a young guy I really wanted to be a successful footballer. The guy who lived over my back fence was the best footballer in the entire district and had played at representative level. He was about 20 years older than me, so I could hardly walk around to his place, knock on the front door and ask him to tell me all the secrets of becoming a successful footballer. What I did do was wait until he came home from work and then purposely kick my footy over his fence. Sometimes I had to climb over and get the thing, but sometimes he would kick it back to me, or even better, sometimes when I climbed the fence he would say, 'Kick it here mate', and that's when he would give me some footy lessons, share with me the things he did and how they worked. Great lessons that helped me play a bigger and better game.

> Make it easy, by learning from those that have been there, done that!

I am sure there are people you already know who have got a promotion, saved some money, learned a second language, lost weight, run a marathon or successfully done something you would like to do. Talk to them; find out what worked well and what they would have done differently if they were starting over.

Three paths to unhappiness

When you take up the challenge of playing a bigger game, you can become frustrated, insecure, stressed out and sometimes quite frantic. There are three paths that put us in this state.

Path 1: expectations

On the first path to unhappiness your expectations don't match your reality. You have some expectations of how things are or should be, but they are completely different from how they really are. When this occurs we start to experience negative emotions—frustration, anger, jealousy, sadness, confusion, a whole heap of emotions—because the two don't match up. Have you experienced these emotions? I bet you have and I guarantee it's because your expectations didn't match the reality.

Most of the misunderstandings between people happen because reality fails to match their expectations. Maybe the expectations you have of your relationship are disappointed. Or the expectation of how you look isn't matched by the reality when you actually look in the mirror. Maybe your role at work falls short of your expectations of the role. In between expectation and reality lies clutter and disappointment. But if you can bring expectation and reality together so they match up, these negative emotions will disappear.

Clarity is the solution. When you clarify both expectations and reality so everyone understands them, you can make the adjustments needed to bring them together as one. There are two ways to achieve clarity. The first is to clarify the expectations of others, understanding what is real to them.

For example, if you are experiencing negative emotions in a relationship, sit down with the person and have an honest discussion. Tell them about the negative emotions you have noticed—the confusion, anger, hurt, jealousy or whatever it is you are concerned about. Then ask the question, 'Why do you think this is happening?' I bet you find there is a difference between what they expect you to do and what you are actually doing, or the way they expect you to behave and the way you actually behave. This is where the disconnect is—between the expectation and the reality. Quite often resolving these issues is really quite simple, and that is what clarity brings to the table. By injecting clarity, you can soon bridge the gap between reality and expectation.

We have dealt with clarity around the expectations of others. Now let's consider our own personal expectations and reality. Imagine you have been waiting a long time for a promotion—head down, bottom up, working away diligently, hoping you will get the next opportunity that crops up. It's not wise to sit in a job telling yourself you want to be the next boss without talking to anyone about your hopes or plans. Maybe there are skills you need that you don't have. You may not even be on the boss's radar yet and no-one knows you want to step up a level. You can't expect to get the next promotion if the reality is that no-one else knows you are even looking for the opportunity.

We need to clarify our expectations, to tell people what we expect and what we really want. When we do this either we win the opportunity we are hoping for or we get some advice on what we need to do differently to create the opportunity in our lives.

So that is the first path to unhappiness—when *our expectations don't match the reality.*

Path 2: comparisons

Imagine I ask you to draw an elephant, and let's assume you have little drawing experience. You do your best and your drawing does quite resemble an elephant. Every time you take a glance at the drawing you feel pleased with yourself. Not a bad effort, you think.

Now imagine that an artist with 20 years' experience displays their drawing of an elephant. The attention to detail is brilliant, the lines, shading, tones—this is a masterpiece. You quietly put your drawing away and tell yourself how hopeless you are.

When I asked you to draw your elephant, you did a reasonable job; it was something you were fairly proud of, until you saw the artist's drawing and compared yours to theirs. The second path to unhappiness is *making comparisons* that are not valid.

If you're out there doing the best you can with the skills and abilities you have, and you're working at your absolute optimum level and you're pretty proud of that, just as you were with your elephant, don't go looking for comparisons. Take stock of where you are, give yourself a pat on the back and then prepare to do even better to play a bigger game.

Take stock of **where** you are, give yourself a pat on the back and then prepare to do even **better**.

I remember taking my wife shopping in Hong Kong; she wanted to buy a watch. We went to a variety of shops looking at watches and she found exactly the watch she wanted. She bargained with the shopkeeper on the price and managed to buy it for $40. It was a great bargain—the same watch at home would have cost $190—so she was really happy with the deal.

I said to her, 'Whatever we do now, we don't look at watches anymore.'

'Why not?' she asked.

'Because you have bought your watch and saved yourself $150. How good is that?'

She couldn't help herself, though, and the next day she visited another shop, where the same watch was priced at $30, without the bargaining! So rather than being content with the fabulous deal she had got and the money she had saved, she was disappointed that she had missed out on an even better deal.

But that's what we do when we start to make comparisons. We become unhappy because we compare our best with someone else's best and that's not what your purpose in life is. It is to compare your best with yourself.

No-one else is going to take responsibility for your life—not your partner, not your parents, not your best friends. No-one is going to take responsibility for how you show up. So it's no good comparing yourself with anyone else but you. If you wake up in the morning and look in the mirror and say to yourself, 'You know what, you're awesome!' then I believe you probably are. Don't go out and compare yourself with someone else. You will not be comparing apples with apples. Stop setting yourself up to fail: just be the best you can possibly be and then work out how you can be even better.

Path 3: judgements

The third path to unhappiness is *making judgements*. Understanding how we make judgements will allow us to play a bigger game. There are several ways we do this.

We judge ourselves

You looked in the mirror this morning and said to yourself, 'Does this shirt go with these jeans? Does my hair look good like this? Do I look okay?'

We judge others

When you walk into a room you make immediate judgements—I like her shoes. He's handsome. She looks young. I like his tie. He looks angry. She looks happy, and so on. All of this in a split second, in the blink of eye. Do you do that?

We make conscious judgements

Conscious judgements are the ones you are aware of when you say, 'I like that jacket'; 'The music is wonderful'; 'These people are helpful'; 'I love my car'; or 'I don't like my house'. These are judgements that we are aware we make, and we are aware of what triggers them.

Being aware of these judgements allows you to redefine them as situations change and you become aware that your judgement or assessment of things has changed as well. It can also be the wake-up call warning you that your thoughts and beliefs can be a bit misguided!

We make subconscious judgements

These are the assessments and judgements we make automatically. For instance, you see someone from a different culture or religious background and immediately make an assessment of what they are like, how they might behave, what is important to them in life. Some (perhaps all) of these judgements may be incorrect. But because we make them without thinking we do not give ourselves the opportunity to question them and can carry them through our entire lives.

When we take complete control of all the judgements we make on all four levels, we have the opportunity to suspend them. This creates new possibilities and opens doors to improved understanding, conversations, relationships and results.

If you are going to fail, fail fast

Let's be honest, raising the bar, pushing the boundaries, stepping up to play a bigger game, means putting yourself out there. On the way you are going to make some mistakes, mess up a bit or even completely stuff up. I am the master of mistakes. If I am going to make a mistake I want to make it as soon as possible. I want to fail fast.

In fact, I find failure valuable, because in these failures are learning opportunities that allow me to improve and get better. You have to dig through a lot of dirt to find the diamonds; I want to get to the diamonds *fast*. So I am prepared to fail, once. I never want to make the same mistake twice. I want to grow and learn from it.

Most of the successful people you know or have heard of (the ones you admire and want to be like), have been rejected, hung up on, turned down; they have missed out, done many things wrong and completely stuffed up; they have been knocked down and got back up again. Many of them have failed their way to success.

Michael Jordan missed 9000 shots and lost 300 games in his career. At critical times he was trusted to take the winning shot and, can you believe it, missed! He failed over and over again, but each time he adjusted and improved and got better and better, until he became the best of the best.

The discovery of penicillin came about through a mistake, Post-it notes were developed out of a failed search for new glue. So when you make a mistake at something, when it all falls apart and you think you're a failure, gather yourself up, dust yourself off, find out where the lesson lies, make the change and get on with playing the bigger game.

Failures are **simply** investments
in your **future** success.

Belinda — the difference clarity makes

Belinda never knew what to expect from her boss. She tried everything to please her but it seemed like the harder she tried, the more disconnected they became. What scared her most was that the gap was growing wider, and you could almost cut the tension between them with a knife.

Belinda was a mess. She slept badly and felt like the whole time she was in the office she was walking on egg shells. She just could not go on this way and was ready to resign from the job entirely.

The final straw was when she was overlooked for a promotion.

A friend of hers had heard me talk at a conference and suggested she have a talk with me. So Belinda came along to one of my events and we discussed what was happening with her boss. Obviously there was a problem and it was getting worse. The only way to sort it out was to get some clarity about what her boss really expected from her. We worked out a strategy for how she could do that without it being intimidating or confronting. Belinda simply requested a performance review—she asked for an hour's one-on-one with her boss in a coffee shop near their office. (This meant an environment that Belinda was comfortable in, and enough time to have a real discussion.) To Belinda's surprise, her boss agreed and the meeting was scheduled.

The secret to overcoming such tensions is to seek clarity, so she asked her boss what exactly were her expectations of Belinda. Her boss replied, 'Well Belinda, to be honest I've been quite disappointed with you [Belinda's heart raced]. You're such a talented and gifted manager, but it frustrates me that you just don't seem to want to go further. Whenever a promotion comes up you never show any interest. I give you projects that clearly show you can do a higher level job, but you never apply.'

Belinda sat back and laughed, which made her boss really uncomfortable. Belinda explained that she had expected to be *offered* a promotion. She thought if she worked hard and was diligent and committed, kept her head down and did her job, she'd be offered a higher position. Then her boss laughed, too.

The difference was amazing. Now they understood each other they got on like a house on fire. Belinda got a promotion and is still with the company today.

If you don't take the time to clarify everyone's expectations and reality, frustrations and disappointments start to mount up and that can only end in disaster.

Chapter 15 summary

⚐ Surround yourself with people who are playing a bigger game.

⚐ Successful people hang out with successful people.

⚐ Find your heroes.

⚐ The three paths to unhappiness are unrealistic expectations, making comparisons and making judgements.

- When expectations and reality are different, disappointment results.

- Don't compare yourself with others; the best person for you to compare yourself with is you.

- Beware of making judgements, both conscious and subconscious.

⚐ Fail fast. Failures are an investment in your future.

MY GAME PLAN:

....

....

....

....

....

....

....

....

....

....

....

....

....

....

....

....

....

....

....

....

....

....

....

....

....

....

....

....

....

....

....

Invest in yourself

If you don't believe in you, how can you expect others to believe in you?

If you ask people what is the biggest investment they ever made, most would probably respond with the item they had spent the most money on—their house or car, a diamond ring or a trip around the world. While these are without doubt big commitments, I believe they are nowhere near the most important investment.

The most important investment you will ever make is in yourself.

Your parents start investing in your growth and development at an early age, sending you off to preschool, primary school and later high school and perhaps university. Throw in the music and dance lessons, sporting pursuits, driving lessons and a host of other expenditures and their investment in you adds up to a fairly large amount.

The **most** important **investment** you will ever make is in yourself.

For some reason, though, once our parents stop investing in us or we have our own children to invest in, we cease investing in ourselves. At that stage most of us spend more money on our lawn—fertiliser, weeding, watering, mowing—than we do on ourselves. It's no wonder we hit a plateau and, in many cases, start to go backwards. Here are some simple, low-cost ways for you to continue to invest in your most important asset—you!

> Any investment in your personal growth, is an investment in your future success!

You could start by spending time with success-minded people. If you don't live with them, find them—they may be hanging out at the gym or on the beach, or involved in special-interest groups or book clubs or personal development courses. Many of them volunteer in their local community—they are out there, you just have to look for them.

And remember how easy it is to connect worldwide today. It will cost you nothing to join groups like LinkedIn, Facebook, Thought Leaders www.thoughtleaderscentral.com and a host of other useful networking sites and forums that will inspire you to achieve more. Get involved in groups online, participate, ask questions, volunteer information. Be proactive: don't wait for things to happen, make them happen.

Don't wait for things to happen, make them happen.

Read books about people who are playing a bigger game, look for the success stories in print or online newspapers. Become curious about the world we live in, search for knowledge, watch the *Discovery Channel*. You will become a more interesting person, your conversation will lift to a whole new level, when you stretch your thinking and expand your networks. Give the following a go:

- Read one non-fiction book every month.

- Swap books, DVDs and CDs with friends. You don't necessarily have to buy new ones all the time.

- Start a mastermind group of go-getters. Not only will you have some lively discussions but you'll expand your networks.

- Invite the most interesting people you know to a barbecue or dinner, and get the conversation going about playing a bigger game.

- Buddy up. Find a friend who loves a challenge and set yourselves some competitive goals that push both of you to achieve more, be more, do more or have more.

- Find someone more successful than you and arrange to have coffee with them. Come prepared with a list of questions you would like to discuss with them. You may be surprised just how generous they are in sharing their experience.

- Find a mentor, a colleague, friend, uncle, aunt or maybe your boss, someone who will give you the right advice and ask the right questions to keep you at the top of your game.

- Do things you don't normally do, challenge yourself, get up and watch the sunrise, walk or ride a bike to work, hike in the mountains, maybe even climb one.

- Clear out your clutter—clothes you haven't worn for more than 12 months, furniture you no longer need, cosmetics, books. Pay a visit to the local St Vinnies or another charity shop and brighten someone else's day.

- Become an expert in something you are passionate about. Expand your knowledge about something you love. Being proactive creates a very positive by-product: happiness.

- Volunteer! During the 2011 floods in Brisbane and Ipswich, we saw an extraordinary movement of very generous people from all over Australia who came with their mops, buckets, brooms and garbage bags to support those affected. They helped total strangers get their lives back on track. In Christchurch after the earthquake and in Japan after the tsunami we witnessed heroic examples of everyday people risking their lives to help those in need.

Some of you might be thinking, what has this got to do with playing a bigger game? How will volunteering at a charity help *me*? If you have never volunteered before, try it. What you might find is:

- You meet amazing people, who are always very positive and great to hang out with.

- You often come away from a volunteering experience feeling incredibly blessed for what you have and aware of how fortunate you are.

- You get to use your skill set in a totally different environment, and this can often really stretch you.

- Playing a bigger game involves lots of different experiences and all of them start with investing in you—growing, stretching, testing your strengths, pushing your boundaries. That's living.

Michael — investing in himself

My mate Michael wanted to start his own business but didn't believe he had the right skills to go out and give it a go. So he whinged and moaned about his job but never did anything about getting his own business off the ground.

Now, I love business, I really enjoy the game of business, creating strategies, business models, marketing plans, sales initiatives. I find it a fantastic adventure. Michael was always asking me for ideas and information, bouncing ideas off me, and telling me what he would do differently if he was running this business or that. He had some fantastic ideas and I was always asking why he didn't just give it a go.

One day he owned up that he just could not bring himself to risk the safety and security of his family by giving up his day job to follow his desire. So I talked to him about how he could have both. Michael loved the game of business just as much as I did. So I suggested that rather than invest money in his own business, why didn't he invest time. He could go to some business networking events or business mastermind groups and share his business ideas. If someone liked the sound of them, he could offer to do some work in their business for a small fee.

By investing his time he could find out (1) if his ideas were good and (2) if someone would pay for them.

Within three months Michael was supplying business coaching to clients after work and on weekends, earning the same money that he was earning in his day job. So he left his old job and now has one of the most successful business coaching practices in my area.

Investing some time for no or very little return produced a massive result for Michael, and now he continues to invest in his growth by committing to a personal learning program each quarter.

Chapter 16 summary

- 👍 The best investment you can make is in yourself.
- 👍 Continual investment in yourself means you're always growing.
- 👍 Connect with people.
- 👍 Do things you don't normally do.
- 👍 Clear out the clutter in your life.
- 👍 Buddy up and compete.
- 👍 Volunteer—it's extremely rewarding.

MY GAME PLAN:

....

....

....

....

....

....

....

....

....

....

....

....

....

....

....

....

....

....

....

....

....

Chapter 17
Be **proud**

So now the ball is in your court. If you truly want to achieve more, I mean *really* want it, if you are determined to be better at something, *heaps* better, if you long to do things you never thought possible, *amazing* things, and if you are absolutely resolved to have more than you ever dreamed of, *much* more, then this book can take you there.

It is truly sad that many people will put this book on a shelf and never look at it again, never put into practice the ideas and activities it introduced them to, never follow through with the inspiration they got from it. Don't let that person be you.

Playing bigger starts with small steps and finishes with giant leaps. I promise you, if you take action, stay committed, and are determined and disciplined, you will be surprised at what happens. You will find yourself turning cartwheels, leaping up and down and shouting to the world, 'YES, I DID IT!'

If you take action, stay **committed**, and are determined and disciplined, you will be **surprised** at what happens.

Success breeds success. When playing a bigger game becomes a daily habit, when you start to look at things and instead of asking yourself 'Why?' you ask 'Why not?', *achieving* more will be easy, *being* more will be a given, *doing* more will become simple and *having* more will be inevitable.

The key to this is *you*. Time and again through this book I have said that you are awesome, and it's true—step into that. I have said that your biggest obstacle is also *you*, so step out of that.

I want you to be proud. I want you to be able to look in the mirror and admire the person you see there. I want you to leave tracks that your children, grandchildren, friends and colleagues will want to follow. Our true measure as individuals is not what we are inspired to be, but whom we can inspire to be like us.

The biggest tragedy right now would be to set this book aside and never open it again, leaving it to gather dust, together with the hopes and dreams and forgotten images of the person you might have been. So keep the book close; read it and reread it; review and rewrite it; immerse yourself in it till your hopes and dreams come true. And then go back to the start and play again.

You cannot go back and **create** a **new** beginning, but you can **start today** and create a new ending.

I look forward to playing a bigger game with you.

[insert your name here]—the story of a successful person

This book is full of the success stories of people I have come into contact with over the years. I hope those personal stories and the rest of the book have inspired you to create your own success story. In fact, I have created one for you—all you need to do is insert your name in the heading above. Here is a little help to get you started on writing your own personal success story...

I am proud. Proud of who I am and what I have done.

I am proud that I have overcome the obstacles and broken through the barriers to achieve what I want to achieve. I have left no stone unturned in my search for what I want out of life. I have not closed the door on any opportunity. I have trusted myself and built a strong belief in what I am capable of and what is possible if I have a strong vision of my future and take action to make it real.

I have discovered that I am not only awesome but absolutely amazing! I serve as an inspiration to others and am proud of the people who follow in my footsteps. I can do without the dream stealers and never make excuses.

I stand up for who I am and what I believe in. I am proud to look in the mirror and face the only person who can really make a difference (me). I am proud of the journey I have been on and the one that lies ahead.

I am proud that when I was challenged to play a bigger game, I grabbed the opportunity with both hands and now I can achieve more, be more, do more and have more than I ever thought possible.

Chapter 17 summary

- The ball is in your court.
- Start with small steps and move on to giant leaps.
- Stay committed, determined and disciplined.
- Look in the mirror and be proud.
- Be an inspiration to others.
- Play a bigger game!

There is no perfect time, to Play A BIGGER Game. Start NOW, in any way you can, stacking small wins on top of each other. In 5 years time, you will be amazed at how far you have come! PLAY BIG!

MY GAME PLAN:

Testimonials

I know everyone in the speaking game and I can tell you, Rowdy McLean knows more about helping people achieve remarkable results. He is the master ast getting people to raise the bar and achieve more than they ever thought possible.
Matt Church, founder of Thought Leaders Global

Rowdy McLean believes in you more than you do, his passion for people and possibilities is simply amazing. I have seen him transform individuals, teams and organisations from lost, stalled and going nowhere to become the absolute peak performers at the top of their game.
Darren Hill, behavioural scientist, Pragmatic Thinking

I have read a heap of books like this before, but none deliver such a simple, commonsense approach to achieving results. The practical tools and real life example are something anybody can identify with and implement. Without doubt the best book of its kind.
Michael Henderson, corporate anthropologist, Cultures at Work

PLAY A **BIGGER** GAME

Free Resources!

If you want to tap into further thoughts on Playing a Bigger Game from Rowdy, here are some great ways to continue the conversation and keep yourself in the best frame of mind to Play a Bigger Game.

Play a Bigger Game Podcast

A weekly podcast full of tips, tricks, ideas and awesome interviews on how you can Play a Bigger Game in your world. Check it out here www.rowdymclean.com/podcasts or you can subscribe to it on iTunes.

Play a Bigger Game on Facebook

Rowdy shares his thoughts, ideas and motivation on how to Play a Bigger game. Find out more at facebook.com/playabiggergame

Play a Bigger Game Blog

This blog features regular articles and videos on how to Play a Bigger Game.

Social media

Connect with Rowdy to get regular Play a Bigger Game updates and stay in touch. Just send a connect request on LinkedIn with the subject Play Bigger. You can also follow Rowdy McLean on Twitter and Instagram

Rowdy

Rowdy McLean

International Keynote Speaker
Motivator
Facilitator
Consultant

Working with Rowdy

As an international keynote speaker Rowdy presents at conferences and events across the globe as well as running 12 month corporate immersions, single- or multi-day masterclasses, executive mentoring programs and facilitating offsite meetings and retreats.

Keynote Topics

Play a Bigger Game–Possibility & attitude

Remarkability–Leaving a positive leadership legacy

Cultural Dynamics–Creating an awesome Company Culture

Simplicity–7 elements of business success

Service Excellence–Differentiation for sustainable success

PLAY A **BIGGER** GAME

Corporate Programs

- Building success driven cultures based on trust commitment and contribution
- Simplifying business strategies to create the very best possible results from minimum inputs
- Taking leaders on the journey from good to great to remarkable while creating a long lasting positive legacy
- Inspiring and motivating individuals to take control of their attitude, opportunities, choices and execution so they can elevate their results
- Creating service excellence driven organisations that stand out in the crowd
- Elevating team trust, communication and execution

Contact

rowdy@playabiggergame.com.au

www.rowdymclean.com

DISCARD

Printed in Australia
19 Apr 2017
628965